BREAKING THROUGH

Leadership Disciplines from Top Performing Staffing Firms

Mike Cleland & Barry Asin

Charted Path Learning Series through Crain Communications Inc.

Copyright @ 2018 by Mike Cleland

All rights reserved, including the right to reproduce this book or portions thereof in any form whatsoever. For information about permissions or special discounts for bulk purchases, send requests to info@chartedpath.com.

Designed by Carrie Wallace Brown
Literary Guidance by Bonnie B. Daneker

Manufactured in the United States of America

ISBN: 978-1-939753-04-5
Library of Congress Control Number: 2017961745

Cleland, Mike and Asin, Barry
Breaking Through: Leadership Disciplines from Top Performing Staffing Firms
1. Leadership 2. Organizational Change 3. Influence (Pyschology)
4. Industrial Organization 5. Strategic Planning 6. Staffing Operations
7. Management 8. Sales 9. Recruiting

To all my clients, past, present, and future, dedicated to building exceptional organizations, and to my family who has always provided me motivation, insight, and support without which this book would not be possible.
MC

To leaders who dare to "break through." And to Amy, Sam, and Julia for their endless support, patience, and good ideas through many staffing industry discussions and stories.
BA

Foreword

Breaking Through is a book I wish I had in 1999, when I was the CEO of a staffing company for the first time. At that time, I had the passion and work ethic for success but an incomplete playbook. Without it, I made more than my share of mistakes. Fortunately, I was given another opportunity when I started Hire Dynamics two years later. Through a lot of hard work, many missteps, and some very tough decisions, we have been fortunate to grow that business to over $100 million in annual revenue.

It was shortly after we launched Hire Dynamics that I met Barry Asin at an SIA event. We hit it off right away. I later got to know Mike Cleland as well and love the fact that I continue to receive "takeaway value" from my interactions with both of them.

Barry and Mike have put together a book that combines the roadmap to success in staffing at every level with both data analytics and the use of storytelling. They are both excellent active listeners who, in addition to their own experiences, have engaged a dozen staffing leaders who have built successful businesses from zero to north of $100 million, to better understand the commonalities that led to their success.

Staffing is a highly competitive business that is full of highs and lows. That is one reason why fewer than 1% of staffing firms achieve $100 million plus. It also is a business that challenges a leader's ability to stay the course or forge into a new opportunity. Several staffing opportunities I pursued got off to a great start and appeared to be the right approach but turned out to be mirages. This book helps you avoid many of the pitfalls that are out there as you build your staffing company. Even if you are not an owner of a staffing company, this book provides great lessons that anyone in staffing management can apply. I also believe many of the lessons here are applicable to other industries (especially those that are business services related).

This book provides insight that can improve your business regardless of your growth stage and ultimate objectives. While Hire Dynamics has achieved the **Breaking Through** status, I have already identified several takeaways from this book for our company. In fact, we have just completed an acquisition that nearly doubled the size of our business, and we are using several of these principles to increase the likelihood of a successful integration.

Breaking Through walks the reader through the disciplines necessary to build a growth business. The staffing industry has proven that there are many different models and strategies that lead to success. The key is being consistent versus constantly reinventing your company. I appreciate how Barry and Mike have identified areas where a company has to find its appropriate balance, whether it is the tension between growth and profitability or the balance between structure and innovation. I personally love learning from others' experiences, and Barry and Mike have done a good job of weaving in real-world examples of how many of the best operators have done it. While I have known many of the individuals interviewed in this book for years, I was pleasantly surprised by the amount of new insights I took away from reading it.

This book also provides staffing executives the gift of self-reflection. Even those who have been successful will find opportunities to improve. In many cases, it reminds me of the old adage, "What got you here won't get you there." I plan to have the entire Hire Dynamics management team read the book and discuss their takeaways and how we can further apply them. It is also a great read and discussion for staffing owner peer groups and for those who have a board of advisors.

Are You Ready?

This chapter is a quality section of the book, with insightful questions for each leadership discipline, but it also raises fair questions for staffing leaders to ask themselves. It will take courage and discipline to self-evaluate your company and personal leadership based on the concepts in this book. Even tougher, it may potentially lead you to make some very hard decisions. The good news is that I am confident that you will develop the most when you are willing to get outside your comfort zone. I encourage each reader to do just that in implementing these concepts.

Finally, I would like to personally thank Barry Asin and Mike Cleland for writing this book and providing a true roadmap for staffing company success. It will certainly only make our industry stronger.

Dan Campbell
Chairman and Founder
Hire Dynamics

Contents

Foreword 5
Introduction 13
Chapter 1: Why Is It So Hard to Grow? 17
   The Staffing Industry Landscape 18
      Trends in Temporary Staffing and Place & Search 21
   The Largest External Barriers to Growth 24
      Competition 24
      Technology—Both Threat and Tool 25
      Regulatory and Legal Barriers 27
   Wrapping Up 28
Chapter 2: The Leadership Mandate 29
   Growth Maturity Model 30
   The Leadership Mandate 41
      The Health of Your Operations 42

    The Leadership Disciplines 46

    Wrapping Up 49

Chapter 3: The Discipline of Commitment 51

    A Tale of Two Leaders 52

    What Is Your Why? 57

    Breaking Through: The Power of Why 63

        Priorities of the Leader 64

        Creating Shared Interest 67

        Impact on Other Leadership Disciplines 68

    Wrapping Up 71

Chapter 4: The Discipline of Direction 73

    Competitive Strategy 76

        What Clients Will You Serve? 77

        What Is Your Value Proposition? 78

    Defining Your Operational Capabilities 81

    Strategic Foresight 83

    Breaking Through: Assess and Adapt 88

        Building an Independent Operation 90

        Achieving Organic Scale 93

        Expanding Your Strategy 97

    Wrapping Up 104

Chapter 5: The Discipline of Culture 107

    Forming a Strong Foundation 111

        Alignment with Competitive Strategy 112

        Shared Beliefs 114

        The Result Focused Team 117

    Breaking Through: Creating Cultural Ambassadors 122

        Building an Independent Operation 124

Contents

    Achieving Organic Scale 127

    Expanding Your Strategy 130

  Wrapping Up 132

Chapter 6: The Discipline of Talent Development 135

  Building a Competitive Team 138

    Assessment 139

    Hiring 143

    Coaching and Performance Management 147

    Promotion 151

  Breaking Through: Elevation and Delegation 157

    Building an Independent Operation 158

    Achieving Organic Scale 161

    Expanding Your Strategy 165

  Wrapping Up 170

Chapter 7: The Discipline of Execution 173

  Ensuring Proper Alignment 177

  Competitive Sales Practices 180

    Small/Medium Buyer 182

    Account Penetration and Management 186

  Competitive Delivery Practices 191

  Breaking Through: Innovate and Replicate 203

    Building an Independent Operation 206

    Achieving Organic Scale 209

    Expanding Your Strategy 212

  Wrapping Up 213

Chapter 8: Are You Ready? 217

  Leadership Disciplines 218

  Wrapping Up 222

Afterword: Breaking Through in Action	223
Acknowledgments	271
About the Authors	273
Mike Cleland	273
Barry Asin	274
Endnotes	275

Introduction

Breaking Through is fundamentally about the central role leaders have in driving growth. We interviewed top-performing staffing leaders and identified the leadership characteristics they have in common. We also explored how these characteristics differ from underperforming firms to better understand the common barriers that prevent most firms from growing. Through both perspectives, we hope to provide practical lessons to help leadership teams grow their business and achieve their goals.

The idea for a book on this topic has a long history. Over the years, we have observed an interesting phenomenon in revenue performance among players in the industry. Of the 19,408 staffing firms operating for a full year in the United States in the latest US Economic Census, almost 85% were below $5 million in annual revenue. In fact, nearly 11,000 staffing firms are under $1 million in revenue, suggesting most are comprised of a solo practitioner or a small handful of staff. Only 657 staffing firms generated more than $25 million in revenue. At the pinnacle of achievement for the industry are a scant 140 firms who made it to the $100 million club of industry top performers, representing only .7% of all staffing firms operating.[1]

Why are some firms breaking through the barriers to growth while others are not? We have been discussing this for years and we saw that the interest from staffing executives was extremely high around how successful firms in the industry were able to grow. Individuals at every level often ask, "What are they doing to be successful?" Knowing that others are interested in learning more about growing their staffing companies, we saw an opportunity to contribute to that ongoing conversation by understanding what high-performing firms were doing that is different from all the rest. We first started talking about turning this research into a book several years ago after discussing the seemingly predictable challenges that all staffing leaders encounter along the path of growth. It was in one of those conversations that we realized we were both acquainted with many leaders who had solved the problem of breakthrough growth and knew from experience what worked in growing a company and what did not.

Our findings are based on decades of industry experience observing high-growth firms as well as firms who have failed to maintain their market share. This book incorporates the extensive industry experience of Charted Path and Staffing Industry Analysts (SIA). Charted Path has consulted with over 75 staffing firms in addition to Mike's experience as an executive in an IT staffing and workforce solutions company. SIA has researched, written about, and hosted events for thousands of staffing firms over nearly 30 years, with Barry's 14 years of experience at SIA incorporating his role as Head of Research and now as President of the organization as well as drawing on his prior experience at Adecco, PepsiCo, and Andersen Consulting.

The goal of our investigation was to discover what these firms have in common and what they do differently from all the rest. In the process of researching this book, we conducted in-depth interviews and focus groups with a dozen fast-growing staffing firms as well as perennial leaders in SIA's Fastest-Growing Staffing Firm report. All the companies we spoke with grew from start-up or nearly start-up mode to being among the leaders in the industry. The companies included in our interviews averaged 21% annual revenue growth[2] (not counting acquisitions) over the past five years, all during a time when market growth was just 5% to 6% annually.[3] This percentage growth is even more impressive when considering that the revenue levels of these companies in many cases now exceeds $100 million.

After all the interviews and discussions, it became apparent to us that there were a number of disciplines in common among the leaders and leadership teams of these businesses. They all were ultimately able to use those disciplines to move from Owner/Operator Dependent businesses to leading mature, sustainable organizations with multiple strategic priorities. Those leaders understood that they must continue to strengthen and sharpen their skills and the skills of their leaders as their business grew.

This book is a compilation of our research and experience, which we hope will provide you important perspectives on leadership in the staffing industry and beyond. This perspective should challenge you and your leadership teams to improve as you learn from some of the successful firms and their inspirational growth stories.

These professionals have given their hearts and souls to create and scale successful staffing businesses. We have also included more stories and advice from them in the Afterword at the back of the book.

We would like to thank the following staffing leaders for sharing their experiences and providing important insights on the nature of leadership in the staffing industry:

Jeff Bowling, The Delta Companies

Dan Campbell, Hire Dynamics

Jay Cohen, Signature Consultants

Mark Eldridge, ALKU

Tom Gimbel, LaSalle Network

Jeff Harris, ettain group

Andrew Limouris, Medix

David Luttrell, AtWork Personnel Services

Marty Luttrell, AtWork Personnel Services

Mark Nussbaum, Signature Consultants

Cindy Pasky, Strategic Staffing Solutions

Ron Shahani, Acro Service Corporation

Leo Sheridan, Advanced Group

While the staffing industry is relatively easy to understand and has few barriers to entry, those who have been around it a while know that it is surprisingly difficult to master. Our hope is that this book becomes a launching pad for your business to **Breaking Through** the barriers between you and even greater success in the future.

Mike Cleland, *Charted Path*
Barry Asin, *SIA*

Chapter 1:
Why Is It So Hard to Grow?

Greatness is not a function of circumstance. Greatness, it turns out, is largely a matter of conscious choice and discipline.
—Jim Collins[4]

Why are there so many staffing firms and yet so few that grow to a substantial size? What gives the leadership of a staffing firm the courage and vision to overcome barriers to growth? What tools or skills do these leaders use to succeed in breaking through barriers to achieve revenue levels of $100 million and beyond? And just what makes them crazy enough to think they can succeed?

These seemingly simple questions have fascinated us over the years. In our roles as advisors to staffing industry professionals, we saw an opportunity to contribute to the understanding of the issues and challenges behind these questions and provide guidance around their surprisingly complex answers. Our findings, presented throughout this book, are based on the extensive industry experience of Charted Path and Staffing Industry Analysts (SIA) observing high-growth firms as well as firms struggling to maintain market share. We also conducted in-depth interviews and focus groups with a dozen fast-growing staffing firms who have managed to grow consistently over the years at rates far exceeding the growth of the industry. In just the past five years, these now mature companies were still able to grow at an average rate of 21% annual revenue growth[5] (not counting acquisitions) at a time when the market grew at just 5% to 6% each year.[6]

The goal of our research was to discover what these firms have in common and what they do differently from all the rest. We examined how fast-growing firms had to lead differently through the various phases of growth. With the information collected for this book, we aim to empower you to achieve rapid, sustainable growth in your staffing business despite the barriers present in today's industry landscape.

The Staffing Industry Landscape

As we discussed in the Introduction, over 19,000 staffing firms operated for a full year in the United States in the latest US Economic Census. Of these, only a scant 140 firms made it to SIA's $100 million club of industry top performers, representing only .7% of all staffing firms operating (Figure 1.1).[7]

What do the firms who were able to grow without the aid of acquisitions do that is different from all the rest? To more closely analyze this, we first need to understand the competitive landscape of staffing. The competitive landscape continues to evolve at an accelerated rate as the pace of technology driven change causes buyers to view the business differently. Regulatory change also impacts the prospects for the industry. Additionally, industries that were previously distinct from staffing have morphed over time, and today the landscape includes not just traditional staffing companies but also related products and services from outside the traditional core staffing business that directly impact the staffing marketplace.

US STAFFING FIRMS BY REVENUE SIZE

Figure 1.1

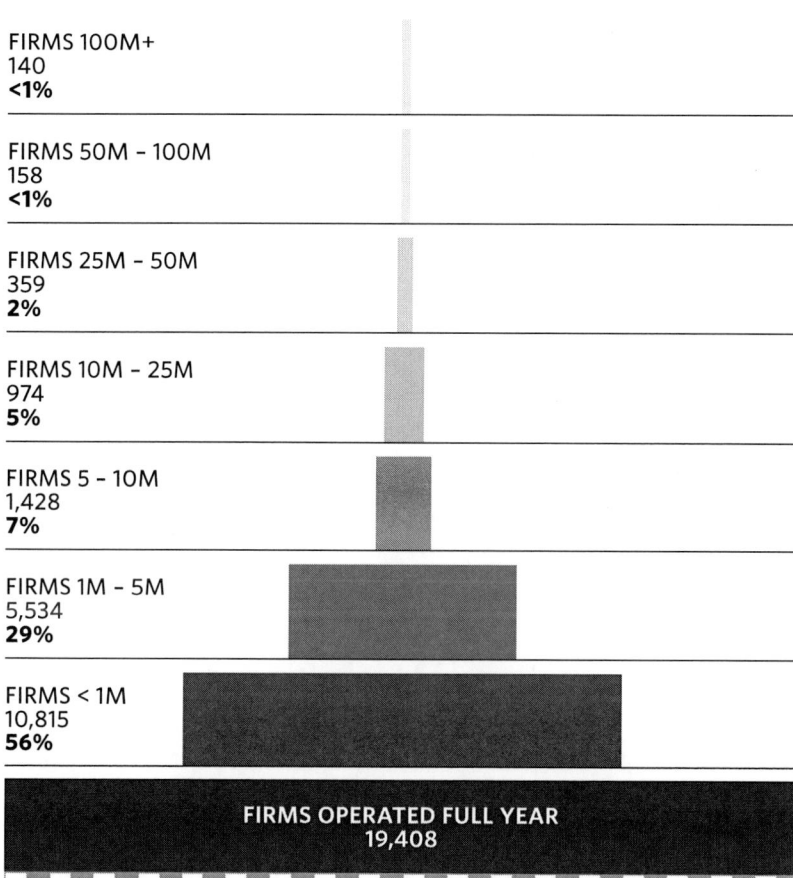

Source: US Census Bureau 2012 Economic Census and Staffing Industry Analysts 2016 Economic Census Update Tool

In its Lexicon of Terms, SIA defines *staffing* as follows:

> *Industry segment of the Workforce Solutions Ecosystem. Major sectors of the Staffing Industry include* <u>Temporary Staffing</u> *and* <u>Place & Search</u> *with the commonality of sourcing workers for a client. Place & Search is comprised of three activities: Direct Hire (or Permanent Placement), Retained Search, and Temporary-to-Permanent Conversions.*[8]

Fortunately, the staffing industry continues to be a solid and growing industry. According to SIA's latest forecast, in 2017, companies in the United States spent $141 billion on staffing services, and global spending on staffing hit $428 billion. The industry in the United States has grown substantially over time. In 1997, total spending amounted to just $74 billion, and in 2007, it hit $121 billion.[9]

This is an important point, as simply growing along with the market is not enough to demonstrate superior performance for a staffing business. Based on SIA's industry forecasts and estimates, the industry achieved a compound annual growth rate of 3.3% between the years 1997 and 2017, including the impact of two major recessions. Consequently, by definition, any firm growing more slowly is losing market share (and therefore not achieving breakthrough levels of performance). For example, if a staffing firm was $10 million in revenue in 1997, to keep up with market growth since that time, it must achieve $19 million in revenue by 2017. Anything less than that is underperforming the market, and even achieving that level indicates a business has been just floating along with market growth rather than exhibiting any unusually strong level of growth.

TRENDS IN TEMPORARY STAFFING AND PLACE & SEARCH

Temporary Staffing and Place & Search involve a third party that recruits workers for clients in place of the clients finding talent themselves. Clients retain staffing firms in part as an outsource play. As they look to focus on their core competence, they shed hiring and management of contingent workers, an activity typically non-core to their business. Clients also appreciate the ability of staffing firms to quickly find and recruit talent in a time of shortage, such as the current "war for talent." Temporary staffing provides organizations with a tool to manage the variability and uncertainty in their demand for labor in a fast-paced, unpredictable business environment. Finally, it should not be discounted that staffing firms frequently take on the role and responsibilities of an employer along with all the risks that decision entails. Employment law and compliance is increasing in complexity, so companies often specifically turn to staffing firms to reduce their risk and help ensure compliance with current changes to relevant laws and regulations.

As companies have grown over time to accept staffing as an effective component of their workforce strategy, the usage of staffing services has grown. This is illustrated by the increase in the penetration rate of temporary labor in the United States workforce, which has grown from around 1% of all workers in the early 1990s to record levels over 2% today. Moreover, the composition of that labor force has become increasingly strategic. Temporary jobs were once viewed as relatively low-skilled secretarial and light industrial workers. Figure 1.2 shows a majority of the spending in the United States today for temporary staffing in terms of dollars is for higher-skilled professionals, in areas like Information Technology, Healthcare, Engineering, and just about any other category of professional jobs that exists.[10]

On the candidate side, the industry has enjoyed growing acceptance of contingent work among the workers themselves, as they come to appreciate that more flexible ways of working often fit their lifestyles. Contingent work can also be a bridge to a traditional job by allowing workers to get their foot in the door at potential employers.

US TEMPORARY STAFFING REVENUE BY SKILL 2017

Figure 1.2

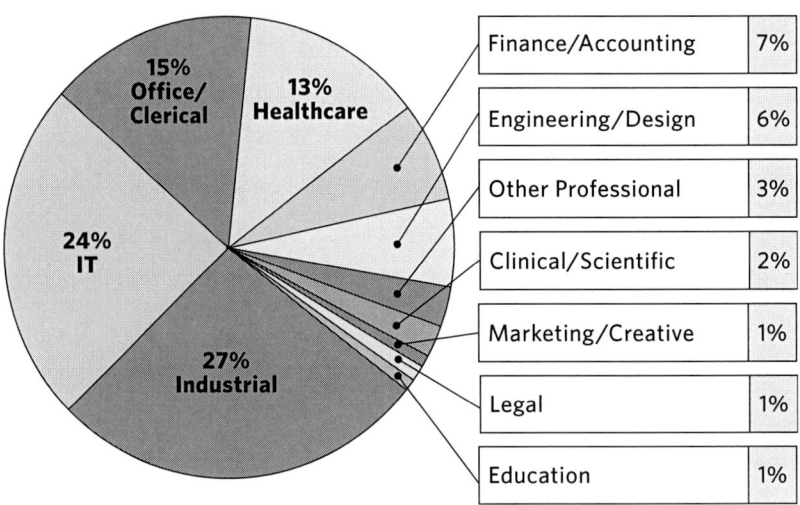

Source: Staffing Industry Analysts, US Staffing Industry Forecast, April 2017 Update.

Illustrating the prevalence of alternative forms of work, SIA estimates that 44 million people in the United States engaged in some form of contingent or "gig" work during 2015, representing 29% of the workforce. SIA sees "'gig work" and "'contingent work" as synonymous, being simply different names for the same phenomenon. Figure 1.3 shows the contingent/gig work that includes temporary workers through a staffing agency, human cloud workers operating through an online platform, independent contractors, directly sourced temporary employees, and Statement of Work (SOW) consultants employed by a consulting firm.[11] There is often surprise at how many people work in these types of nontraditional jobs.

NUMBER OF US WORKERS BY WORK ARRANGEMENT 2015
Figure 1.3

2015 WORK ARRANGEMENT	# OF WORKERS (MILLION) THROUGHOUT THE YEAR	% OF ALL WORKERS
Temporary Workers Assigned Through Staffing Agency[a]	9.5	6.2%
Human Cloud Workers	9.7	6.4%
IC/Self-Employed With No Employees[b]	23.5	15.5%
Temporary Employees Sourced Directly	5.5	3.6%
SOW Consultants Employed by Consulting Firm	2.9	1.9%
Total US Contingent Workforce[c]	**44.1**	**29%**

Source: Staffing Industry Analysts, Measuring the Gig Economy: Inside the New Paradigm of Contingent Work, August 2016.

[a] Represents everyone who worked during the course of the year in one of these roles. Thus, while approximately 2% of the workforce are working at a staffing agency on any given day, during the course of the year approximately 6.2% of workers work for a staffing agency at some point.

[b] Excludes 1099/self-employed workers already reported as temporary agency or human cloud workers.

[c] The sum of estimates from each of the five categories totals to more than 44 million, as a person could go on a temporary assignment through a staffing agency and could also take a gig through the human cloud. Within our estimates, a person that did both counts in each category, but only counts as one contingent worker.

Given the large numbers of people working in contingent/gig work, it is not shocking that many prefer that as a form of work. SIA surveys suggest that approximately 53% of temporary agency workers prefer some form of alternative work arrangement (including 22% that prefer part-time work) over a traditional full-time job. Among independent contractors, the preference is even more dramatic, with 69% preferring to run their own business or work as an independent contractor/freelancer.[12]

The Largest External Barriers to Growth

While the staffing industry has been a good place to grow a business, there are still many challenges and barriers to growth that exist outside of any one staffing firm's control. These can include competition, technology, and cultural and legal impediments. The best preparation to react to these is to become familiar with them, plan strategies to overcome them, and regularly keep updated on the external activity.

COMPETITION

Chief among these barriers to growth is competition. Staffing is an intensely competitive business, and as a result, it is highly fragmented. Figure 1.4 details SIA's annual ranking of staffing's largest firms and no one company has significant market share. This fragmentation means high levels of competition, making it difficult for staffing firms to even retain existing customers, much less grow into serving new customers. It also means there is extensive opportunity for all who are interested if they have the right strategy in place and execute well on it.

A wide array of related industries and services can and do encroach on the business traditionally served by staffing firms. SIA defines the ecosystem around Staffing as the Workforce Solutions Ecosystem as seen in Figure

1.5. For those interested, there is a free report explaining the ecosystem on SIA's website at www.staffingindustry.com in the "Resources" section.

LARGEST STAFFING FIRMS IN THE UNITED STATES BY 2016 REVENUE
Figure 1.4

RANK	COMPANY	2016 US STAFFING REVENUE ($ million)	MARKET SHARE
1	Allegis Group	8,928	6.5%
2	Randstad Holding	4,674	3.4%
3	Adecco	4,597	3.4%
4	Robert Half International	3,546	2.6%
5	Kelly Services	3,402	2.5%
6	Manpower Group	3,315	2.4%
7	Express Employment Professionals	2,977	2.2%
8	EmployBridge Holding Company	2,950	2.2%
9	TrueBlue	2,510	1.8%
10	On Assignment	2,325	1.7%

Ranked by estimated 2016 US staffing revenue
Source: Staffing Industry Analysts, Largest Staffing Firms in the United States: 2017 Update, July 2017.

TECHNOLOGY—BOTH THREAT AND TOOL

These workforce solutions represent a potential threat (as well as opportunities for growth) to players in the industry. Over the past several decades, these businesses have interacted with and, in some cases, disrupted the staffing industry. The classic example of this disruption has been the introduction of Vendor Management Systems (VMS) technology that has greatly increased transparency between staffing firms and their large enterprise clients and enabled the rise of Managed Service Providers (MSPs) who outsource the management of entire contingent workforce programs. The use of VMS has put pricing pressure on staffing firms and driven change in the industry while also positively increasing the overall level of spending on staffing services by large clients utilizing these tools.[13]

WORKFORCE SOLUTIONS ECOSYSTEM

Figure 1.5

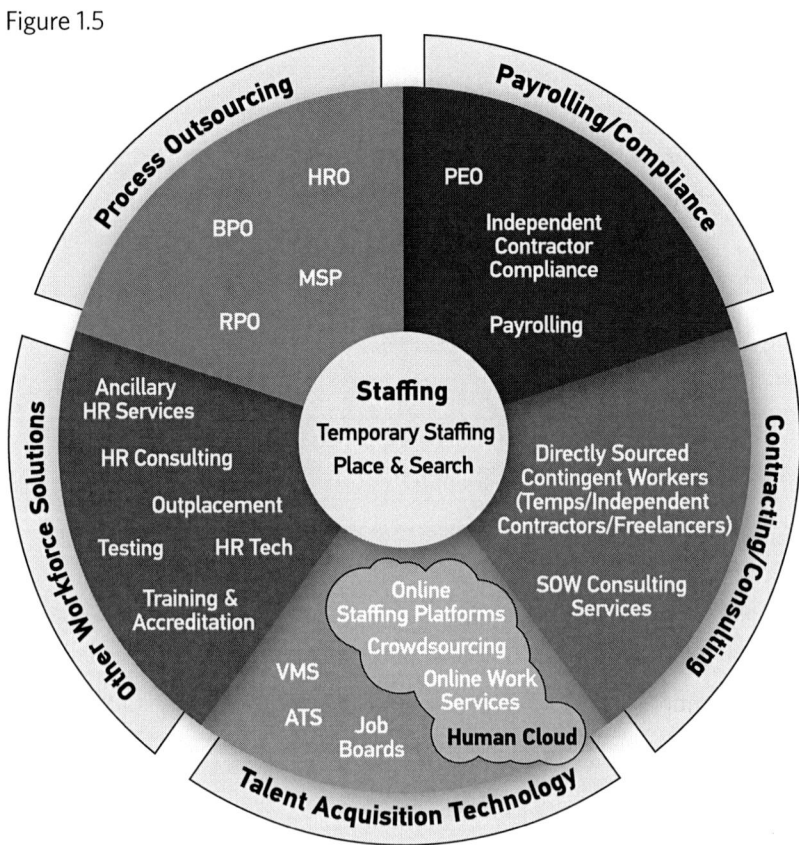

www.staffingindustry.com | ©2017 Crain Communications Inc.

The Workforce Solutions ecosystem includes Temporary Staffing and Place & Search at its core. These core areas are surrounded by a variety of industries that are broken into sectors, including process outsourcing such as MSPs, Payrolling/Compliance, Contracting/Consulting, Talent Acquisition Technology including VMS and Online Staffing, and other Workforce Solutions. Of particular note in terms of growth over the past several years has been the rise of the Human Cloud and Online Staffing, which utilize web-based platforms to directly connect workers and hiring managers, with little or no human intervention in the process. Over the long-term, these systems represent a threat to the growth of staffing firms, as they innately lower costs and put pressure on traditional staffing models, though the models they utilize are also an opportunity for staffing firms interested in innovation.

REGULATORY AND LEGAL BARRIERS

Finally, regulatory and legal impediments may hamper growth in staffing. The infamous Microsoft decision from the 1990s still undermines confidence in, and therefore limits expansion of, contingent labor. In this case, a number of Microsoft contractors were ultimately judged to be de facto employees of Microsoft and entitled to Microsoft benefits, including stock options. While the specific situation that happened in this case can now easily be corrected through adjustment of benefit plan language, the concerns about "co-employment" and perceived risks of using temporary or other contingent workers continue to linger.

Today more concern is found around the risk of independent contractor misclassification, as companies fear that their independent contractors could be reclassified as employees and thus have the company liable for back taxes, benefits, and penalties. All these concerns and other regulatory issues dampen the demand for staffing services and provide an external barrier to growth for staffing firms, though at times, increased employment regulation can also drive demand for staffing services as clients seek to outsource the complexity inherent in taking on the role of employer.

Wrapping Up

As we review the competitive landscape of the staffing industry, it is apparent that competition is fierce and the barriers to growth are real. While all external factors are important influencers, we believe that *internal* barriers are the primary reason that most staffing firms fail to grow.

In the coming chapters, we will explore the disciplines and practices of breakthrough leaders as they address these internal barriers in more detail. The leadership journey is not easy, and there are many possible missteps, but we believe there is a path to success that can maximize the odds of breakthrough growth for your business.

Chapter 2:
The Leadership Mandate

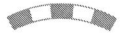

*Excellent firms don't believe in excellence—
only in constant improvement and constant change.*
—Tom Peters[14]

After a couple years of intense start-up activity, George, a small staffing firm CEO, had reached a level of success. He was happy with the volume of customers and the lifestyle the business afforded him and his team. His energies went into maintaining the current customer base, keeping the team happy, and doing the sales and recruiting work that he loved.

The only problem for George was that the external world did not cooperate. Slowly over time, his business began to be eroded by new competitors, new technologies, and changes in the needs of his key clients. One day he woke up to discover that his largest customer had gone out to bid for a new supplier and was pulling their business away from George's firm. While George would have been happy with a firm that stayed the same size for many years, he now had a business that was in a state of decline and in need of a turnaround.

While the details are imaginary, we see stories like this taking place every day in the staffing industry, where firms with very similar market positions, customers, and reputations make very different choices about the future of their business. Time and time again, we see that regardless of growth goals, leaders must adapt and mature to maneuver through the ever-shifting competitive landscape. If status quo thinking dominates, leadership development stops. Company stagnation and operational weakness will inevitably follow. If you want your company to survive, much less grow, there is no standing still.

While George may represent the worst-case scenario, his story does capture the consequences of complacency in a hypercompetitive world of staffing. Your company needs leaders who are never satisfied with the status quo and are always looking for ways to make the company more competitive. This linkage between growth and leadership was validated in our research, leaving us with the conclusion that *the biggest predictor of staffing company success is the effectiveness of the leadership team.*

Your role in driving growth is largely defined by what the company needs based on its size and operational maturity. The Growth Maturity Model provides important perspective both on where your company is and what needs to change for it to continue to grow. This perspective will provide you greater clarity of the scope of change that is required of you and your key leaders to help you determine whether you are truly committed to growing your company.

Growth Maturity Model

Long-term growth is not linear or predictable. Instead, growth typically follows a pattern of accelerated expansion followed by a plateau or even a period of top-line contraction. These plateaus are not just a reflection of the external marketplace or the loss of a single client. Instead, these plateaus represent a growth ceiling driven largely by operational limitations—a ceiling that can only be broken by fundamentally transforming how the organization is led. For this reason, the severity of the plateaus and the ability to reach the next phase of accelerated growth is largely dependent on the leadership team being aware of their weaknesses and making the necessary changes.

Unfortunately, self-reflection is not how most of us respond to failures. However, to be an effective leader, that is where you should begin.

I remember being $3 million in revenue and wondering how we were going to get to $20 million. And the same thing happened when we were at $25 million trying to get to $50 million. And even as we were approaching $100 million, we started to see the steam coming out of the pipes and we knew that we had to do things differently.

As a founder, you always have to be wondering whether you are the person to lead the organization to the next level. You cannot be the same CEO you always were. You have to transform yourself. I have the mentality that the people who got me here are not necessarily going to get me to the next level. That includes looking at myself. You have got to be willing to make those tough decisions, all the way down, even to the people who were there with you from day one.

—Jeff Harris, ettain group

Executives of top-performing companies understand that leaders are responsible for ensuring not only that daily operations are running effectively but also that the operations are making the necessary changes to scale and remain competitive. The ability to efficiently scale operations through gradual transformation requires awareness and discipline, but is central to being able to achieve sustainable growth.

The good news is that these are factors leadership can control. The bad news is that they require skills, discipline, and knowledge that leadership has typically never used or simply does not have. This gap challenges the entire leadership team, but the challenge begins with the chief executive. Is growth worth the personal sacrifice? How much risk am I willing to take? Am I willing to change how I lead? The challenges of a growing company demand answers to those questions, and the answers largely determine whether a company stagnates or breaks through.

GROWTH MATURITY MODEL

Figure 2.1

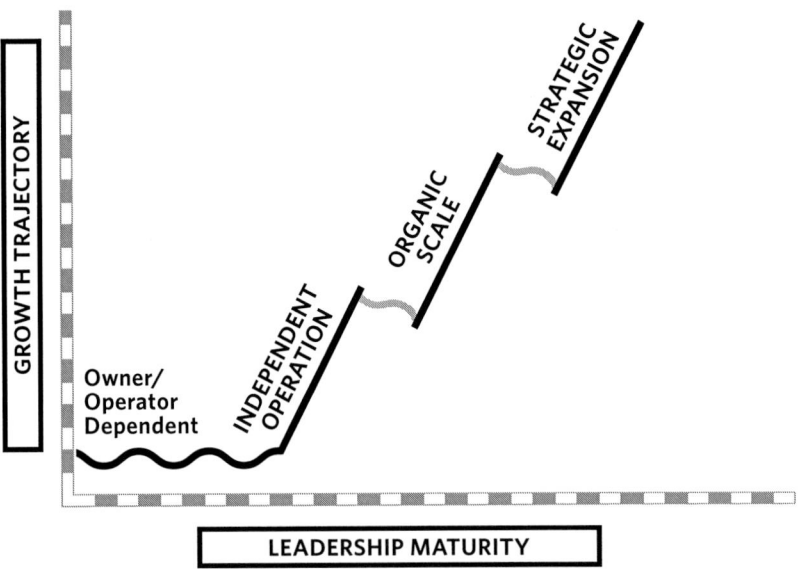

In Figure 2.1, we have a visual representation of the phases of growth. The x-axis represents Leadership Maturity, which is defined by the amount of complexity the leadership team can profitably scale. The y-axis represents the Growth Trajectory, which is a series of growth spikes followed by plateaus, creating distinct phases. This pattern is driven by the ability of the management team to keep up with the increasing complexity of a growing organization. As a company grows, it becomes more complex to manage. This complexity eventually outpaces the maturation of the leadership team, causing a plateau in growth. What we have found is that companies reach these plateaus at distinct phases of operational maturity: Owner/Operator Dependent, Independent Operation, Organic Scale, and Strategic Expansion.

Another perspective on the Growth Maturity Model is highlighted in the classic *Harvard Business Review* article on "Evolution and Revolution as Organizations Grow" by Larry E. Greiner.[15] In that article, Greiner discusses the phases of growth companies typically go through that often end in a crisis, which if successfully resolved, then leads to the next stage of growth. While the phases are focused on staffing operations, the concept holds true to all industries. Below is a brief description of each phase.

Owner/Operator Dependent Phase

At this phase, staffing firms are dependent on the Owner/Operator who plays the role of producer, line-level manager, and chief executive. Many Owner/Operators choose to stay at this phase since it can provide a healthy income without the risks and stress of a growing company. The Owner/Operator is heavily involved in production, most often on the sales side of the business. They also hire, train, and manage the personnel as well as running the back office. The organization is built to maintain its current state versus growth. The long-term success of the company is based largely on the talents of the Owner/Operator along with its minimal cost structure and adaptability versus a scalable growth strategy.

The primary vulnerability in this phase is that the day may come when the Owner/Operator can no longer, or will no longer, perform all the functions that are required of them. The success or failure of the company truly lies in their daily involvement. Extended absence or neglect threatens the very existence of the company.

In some cases, the company begins to experience accelerated growth typically driven by increased demand from legacy accounts. This increase in demand forces the hand of the chief executive. They must either invest in attempting to keep up with demand or ignore the opportunity. The leaders who choose to invest may start by growing the delivery team to meet current demand. Others who are even more aggressive begin hiring salespeople to take on account management responsibilities. It is these founders who have made the first step in building an Independent Operation because production is gradually being delegated away from the founder and given to the team. This fundamentally changes the role of the founder. The founder now must focus on creating a team of well-trained individuals who can independently collaborate.

As Ron Shahani of Acro Service Corporation states, this transition changes the fabric of the company and creates the foundation to become an Independent Operation.

Once we were in the $5 to $10 million in revenue range, I realized that if we were to continue to scale the business, we would need to nurture people more, encourage their ideas, become better listeners, and be more participative. That, along with a more team oriented decision making style, was the key to our growth.

—*Ron Shahani, Acro Service Corporation*

Independent Operation Phase

The Independent Operation phase is achieved when a business can grow without the daily involvement of the chief executive. By this phase, many of the day-to-day leadership responsibilities have been delegated. Often these leaders are promoted internally and groomed by the chief executive. Internal promotion ensures consistency and helps minimize disruption. In other cases, leaders are brought in from the outside, potentially bringing greater expertise at the risk of more disruption. Regardless of the approach, the day-to-day leadership responsibilities are delegated away from the chief executive to leaders who can manage a single location and/or operation.

As the company enters this phase, it becomes more difficult for the chief executive to manage the business. Problems with communication, employee morale, and operational inefficiencies become more common. In addition, the chief executive has less visibility as the team grows, complicating problem solving. If the chief executive continues to manage the same way, they may implement misguided solutions that not only do not solve significant problems but also further disrupt the organization, making problems worse.

This presents a crossroads for chief executives. For the business to continue to grow, they must now be willing to delegate decision making to other leaders and implement some structure to their organization. Leadership delegation represents a significant leap of faith for many executives, but they understand that leadership stagnation is now the greatest threat to growth. If the executive does not change, the company will never be able to grow past the individual's limitations and become truly independent.

The importance of developing independent leaders is stressed by Jay Cohen of Signature Consultants.

We were always driven by growth and always investing to build the business. That meant from the beginning that we knew we had to build a team and could not do it alone. Early on, we hired a couple of young salespeople to drive our growth and brought them in with what would be considered an industry standard sales compensation package joined with a commitment to share the company's upside in the event of a sale. That economic arrangement, combined with an empowered leadership model and, of course, their talents, made all the difference. They essentially ran the business on a day-to-day basis and allowed us to grow without daily involvement from me and my partners.

—Jay Cohen, Signature Consultants

As the Independent Operation grows, competitive practices are implemented to provide the necessary structure. These competitive practices are then tested and refined to where they become a proven part of the execution of the company strategy. At this point, these practices can be replicated, preparing the organization for Organic Scale.

Organic Scale Phase

Organic Scale is the ability to replicate the Independent Operation while achieving profitable growth. To accomplish Organic Scale, additional layers of management between the executives and the field must be added, which requires structural changes to the organization. These changes allow decision making to be further delegated, giving remote offices a level of autonomy and, at the same time, ensuring they are effectively executing the company strategy and receiving support from the top to do so.

As the line-level leadership team matures the organization, it gains the ability to add sales and recruiting resources while maintaining production standards. At this level, investment in infrastructure (as well as processes and procedures) allows competitive practices to be replicated, letting operations become more turn-key. This increased sophistication typically enables rapid expansion into new marketplaces.

Marketplace expansion can be achieved through a variety of structures, including a central location, local branches, or a hybrid that includes sales offices supported by a central delivery center. How the company decides to scale is based primarily on a well-defined growth strategy that focuses investments and defines the needed operational capabilities. Regardless of the approach, the business at this stage becomes exponentially more complex and challenges the leadership team to evolve once again. The founder now must choose to become a dedicated chief executive or hire someone who can handle the new challenges associated with a larger firm.

The growth of the company depends on the ability of the chief executive and top leadership to scale and develop high-quality leadership talent. The complexity of the business demands that these leaders become both good tactical managers and strategic problem solvers, collaborating with their peers to address the more complicated problems that come with a larger organization. Over time, some leaders thrive and become more self-sufficient. These leaders will continue to develop, taking on greater and greater responsibilities, thus enabling the company to grow. Other leaders will struggle to develop and fall further and further behind, leaving the chief executive with the difficult task of replacing loyal employees whose roles have outgrown their abilities.

In this phase, firms rely on more sophisticated data reporting to provide insight into the sales and recruiting team, often referred to as the "production" team, as well as branch operations. Company-wide standards become a priority to ensure consistency on how production personnel are managed. In addition, predictive analytics are used to forecast when further investment in staff is needed as well as when a branch may need corrective action. With data-driven decision making, policies and processes become better defined and standardized to provide greater structure on how teams collaborate on problems that impact the entire company.

Without that structure, it becomes more and more difficult to roll out solutions that achieve buy-in from the remote branches as highlighted by Mark Eldridge of ALKU.

We had to get smart to go from Organic Scale to Strategic Expansion. We had a bunch of smart people, but we did not have a group consciousness. We did not know who we were as a company and how we approached problems. We needed to have everything written down, so we now have a seven step process for problem resolution. We have it written down, and we all know it. Whenever there is a problem, we know how we are going to approach it. We follow the process, and it works.

—Mark Eldridge, ALKU

In the Organic Scale phase, cash management becomes a key concern. Many of the companies we studied had very little capital injected in the Owner/Operator phase. Since most were growing organically rather than by acquisition, cash flow was often the principal limitation on how fast they could hire internal staff and expand their operations. Unlike many other industries, staffing firms do not require a large initial investment if operated successfully. As a company grows, the executives must ensure that cash is collected fast enough to both meet payroll and invest in additional internal staff. Today there are many good options that staffing owners have available to finance temporary payroll and accounts receivable. For firms with a growth mindset, having that financing is crucial to move quickly to the next level of growth. Without some financial cushion, the odds of breaking through to the next level of growth are dramatically lower. This is especially true during the Organic Scale phase, which requires upfront investments to ramp up new operations.

After an organization has mastered replicating operations while maintaining profitability, leadership is prepared to look at other strategies to drive long-term growth. We will examine that as part of Strategic Expansion.

Strategic Expansion Phase

Strategic Expansion happens when companies pursue growth either through acquisition or the addition of service offerings. Companies that reach a level of operational maturity where branches are largely self-sufficient and profitable are best suited for this phase. This self-sufficiency and profitability provide the executive team the time and capital necessary for the difficult work of executing on multiple strategies simultaneously. Strategic Expansion opportunities include aggressive acquisitions, new staffing verticals, or new strategic service offerings, such as Recruitment Process Offering (RPO) or MSPs.

In some cases, Strategic Expansion occurs before the company has become efficient at Organic Scale; however, the risks associated with doing so are significant. If the operations are not self-sufficient or profitable, the distraction and needed investment required from the new strategy pulls time and financial resources away from the core business, further weakening it. Regardless, risks can be mitigated by first selecting a strategy that is closely adjacent to the core business, which will be discussed in Chapter 3.

Cindy Pasky of Strategic Staffing Solutions knew her company was primed for expansion. She pursued adding service offerings within her current client base, staying close to her core operations. This allowed Cindy to leverage both her team's knowledge of those accounts and the strong relationships she had built with their key decision makers. The expansion was a successful advancement of the strategic decision Cindy had made years earlier: Focus on large accounts in specific industry verticals and become a knowledgeable partner to provide a higher level of service to them as their relationship developed over time.

> *Our assumption was that there is always a market and you have to define it; you cannot let it define you. We decided we were going to develop customer relationships within the finance industry as well as the healthcare, insurance, and energy industries as our starting core. Having that in-depth knowledge of our industry and of our customers helps to open doors for us. Understanding the customers' needs allowed us to develop our staff augmentation, direct hire recruiting, workforce programs, and outsourced solutions practices.*
>
> —*Cindy Pasky, Strategic Staffing Solutions*

An argument can be made that there are firms that achieve relatively high revenue numbers without also seeing increased maturity of the leadership team. Does that disprove the relationship between leadership maturity and growth? While there are exceptions to every rule, we are confident the answer is no. In the Growth Maturity Model (Figure 2.1), revenue was left off the chart intentionally. While there is a correlation between revenue and operational maturity, it is dangerous to assume that just because a firm is at a particular revenue level, it has reached a certain level of maturity and that revenue level is sustainable.

For example, organizations exist that generate $70 million in revenue but have a lot of the characteristics of an Owner/Operator company, and there are $20 million organizations that are in the Organic Scale phase. One difference is that in the future, the former will likely experience contraction due to a crisis in its leadership development, while the latter will more likely be able to achieve long-term sustainable growth.

Short-term growth can be achieved with relatively low operational maturity. However, it will most likely not be sustainable. Therefore, buyers of staffing companies take the strength of the entire management team into account when deciding whether to pursue a firm—as well as determining how much they are willing to pay for it. Organizations with strong management teams are highly valuable, whereas those who are dependent on the Owner/Operator are very difficult to sell or will sell with lower valuations. The relationship between sustainable company growth and leadership creates an important mandate for chief executives and leaders at all levels. It is a mandate that must be embraced in order to break through.

The Leadership Mandate

If you want to maintain or grow your business, you must commit to the growth of yourself and your team. This is the essence of the leadership mandate.

Effective leadership teams enable a firm to scale more efficiently and take market share from lesser competitors. It is this ability to consistently take away market share that allows their companies to grow at rates far above the industry average. This direct relationship between leadership effectiveness and accelerated growth generally holds true regardless of company size, market segment, or any other variable.

The impact of ineffective leadership is often underestimated or ignored simply because the negative consequences can take years to manifest themselves. This lesson is not obvious, particularly during years of economic growth, when the company may grow at a respectable clip even though the organization is becoming less and less competitive.

Growth tends to lull leadership into a false sense of security, the assumption being that if the company is growing, it must be fundamentally healthy. However, the drivers of growth are often random and opportunistic and do not reflect the level of operational health or competitiveness. Without effective leadership, systemic issues will eventually develop and become so severe that they can undermine a company dramatically and threaten the long-term survival of the business. Even before considering where you are on the Growth Maturity Model (Figure 2.1), you should diagnose whether your operations are healthy—whether you have systemic weaknesses that can inhibit growth or, in some cases, reduce your market share.

THE HEALTH OF YOUR OPERATIONS

Systemic weaknesses can develop when leadership ignores the mandate to grow. Common systemic weaknesses include sales atrophy, operational stagnation, and financial deterioration. It is important to keep in mind that these systemic issues are often hidden and gradually build over time. Their insidious nature makes them difficult to detect until they reach critical mass and begin impacting company performance.

One reason for this is that they are often misdiagnosed as simply personnel problems. While staff do play an important role, they are often a symptom of systemic weaknesess, not the cause. When this happens, leadership focuses unduly on firing and hiring employees. This approach can lead to high turnover, with only a small minority of exceptional people achieving their goals. High turnover also results in severely damaged customer and candidate relationships, ultimately leading to the loss of business. Therefore, it is critical to ensure there are no major systemic weaknesses underlying poor performance. If systemic issues are present and you identify them, quick and decisive actions to address them will increase the likelihood of employees becoming productive and avoid the cycle of unnecessary turnover and loss of business.

Sales Atrophy

For many companies, rapid growth is driven by large account penetration. While these large accounts are driving growth, it is easy to forget the hard work of business development and account management that came beforehand. Over time, these accounts can continue to produce even while the sales organization becomes more complacent. The lack of new accounts weakens the recruiting team because they are only exposed to a smaller variety of roles from the same companies. The organization reduces its focus on sales and becomes more internally focused until the inevitable happens: the legacy accounts shrink or go away. At this point, the staffing firm not only has lost a large portion of its revenue but also has unwittingly lost the sales capabilities that allowed it to land and establish the accounts in the first place.

Rebuilding sales capabilities is a complex problem to overcome because it often requires successfully executing three very difficult initiatives: new hiring, extensive training, and a fundamental cultural reset. From a hiring perspective, it is not uncommon for the existing sales team to fail to make the transition, necessitating the hiring of new people to supplement or replace them. In addition, the training that occurs organically in an aggressive sales organization is often lost, requiring the development of a training program and/or the hiring of a capable sales leader. Culturally, leaders must shift the team's perspective away from internal distractions to external opportunities where everyone now sees sales as the top priority. This requires the team to leave the predictability and comfort of legacy accounts for the harsh world of new business development, where both sales and recruiting have to outwork the competition. Keep in mind, this new reality can test the mettle of both recruiting and sales, and it can lead to increased turnover.

Operational Stagnation

Organizations, by their nature, generally do not want to change. Conversely, the market demands that staffing firms be adaptable to survive. As outlined in the previous chapter, we live in a competitive landscape that is constantly shifting. The changes brought on by technology alone force operational changes in how staffing firms sell, recruit, and run their back office. Some companies leverage these changes to gain a competitive advantage. Others adopt change more gradually but still invest in their operations to remain competitive, while some fall behind.

Operational improvements include any internal change to strengthen company competitiveness. For companies that are actively responding to the changing landscape, these improvements can be incremental and relatively minor, such as new tools or tweaks to key processes, policies, and/or roles and responsibilities.

However, organizations that have been neglecting their operations for a long period of time often find themselves so far behind the competition that radical change is needed to keep the company competitive. Just with sales, these radical improvements can take months to implement and, at times, well over a year to see a desired return. These include entirely replacing front-office or back-office software, reengineering entire workflows, and sometimes an aggressive restructuring of the organization.

Deteriorating Financial Health

The seduction of short-term growth can lead executives to work with clients who can put them out of business. Typically, this is not the intent of the client, but it is a predictable result of a combination of poor strategy, desperation, and dependence. These are not just clients who have onerous financial terms; there are also clients who require a large operational investment to service an account. One common example of these types of clients is large accounts that have Service Level Agreements (SLAs) requiring that staffing firms attempt to fill all jobs, have low job order close rates, and have submittal-to-hire ratios that are north of 50 to 1. In addition, there can be costly background screening, volume discounts, and laborious administrative processes/paperwork adding to the cost of placements. There are very few staffing firms that can support this kind of business effectively, yet the desire to increase revenue often traps staffing firms into programs that drain bottom-line profitability.

There is always a level of tension between growth and profitability that the executive must balance with a clear vision. If an executive prioritizes too much on profitability, this will tend to negatively impact revenue growth because the team will become more selective about the business they pursue. If an executive prioritizes growth, this will tend to negatively impact the financial health of the company because the team will pursue unprofitable business. While the former may temporarily sacrifice growth, the latter can threaten the company's long-term financial viability. The solution is knowing what the proper balance is for your situation.

In addition to reduced profitability, another equally important impact on financial health is poor diversification of gross profit dollars. Organizations that are not sales driven may eventually focus on fewer and fewer accounts. Over time, this creates an unhealthy consolidation of gross profit within too few accounts, leaving the company financially vulnerable to the whims of a handful of key decision makers.

Sales atrophy, operational stagnation, and deteriorating financial health are all systemic issues you must fight in your company to survive an increasingly competitive landscape. However, simply addressing these issues is not enough to break through barriers to growth. Leaders of rapidly growing companies have additional challenges related to that growth, which also must be addressed. To address these complexities, growth requires continuous maturation of specific leadership disciplines from the chief executive down to the line-level manager.

THE LEADERSHIP DISCIPLINES

The Leadership Mandate stresses the link between leadership maturity and rapid sustainable growth. However, the mandate is meaningless unless we can answer the question of what it means to be an effective leader in the staffing industry. The Leadership Disciplines provide an answer to that question by looking at how leadership impacts both strategic and tactical drivers of company growth. Through our observations and discussions with top-performing staffing leaders, we have identified five consistent disciplines embraced by these business leaders.

FIVE LEADERSHIP DISCIPLINES

Figure 2.2

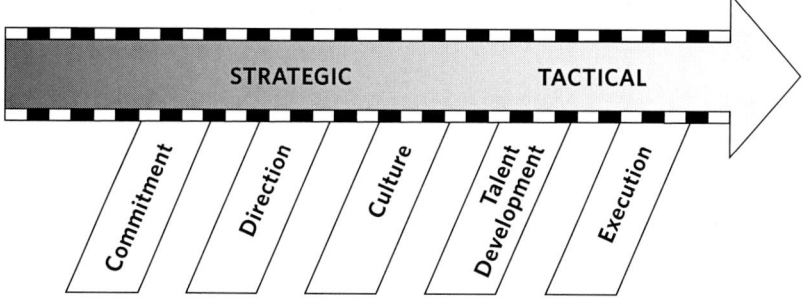

As seen in Figure 2.2, we believe there are five disciplines that high-performing staffing firms have in common. The disciplines on the left are more strategic, and they become more tactical as they move to the right. The more strategic Disciplines of Commitment and Direction answer the questions "Why do we exist?" and "What problems do we solve?" The Disciplines of Talent Development and Execution focus on the tactical question of "How do we solve those problems?" The Discipline of Culture sits between them since it partially answers why, what, and how. In addition, each discipline influences the others to some extent.

Below you will find a brief description of each discipline. The dynamics between the leadership disciplines will be discussed in later chapters.

Commitment

The foundation of breaking through is built on leadership's commitment to build an exceptional company. Leaders who have the Discipline of

Commitment are determined to grow and are willing to make the necessary personal and professional sacrifices that while often painful in the short-term, are required for the business to achieve its long-term objectives. This commitment to growth is based on building an organization that is aligned with the personal values and priorities of the founder. For many founders of top-performing firms, growth is more than hitting a financial number; it is an integral part of their personal and professional legacy.

Direction

The Discipline of Direction is comprised of a clear company vision that is accompanied by a compelling strategy and supported by well-aligned operations. As a company grows, the Discipline of Direction includes the ability to adapt the organization in an increasing fluid and complex environment.

Culture

A focus on building a Performance-Driven Culture by design rather than by default was common across our top-performing staffing leaders. Most of the leaders we interviewed felt that their strong culture is a major competitive differentiator. Of course, culture has many facets and is difficult to define. At its core, we believe culture is a combination of a shared belief system and a common goal. Culture provides the unwritten rules of team behavior and plays a large role in defining how teams collaborate and focus on results.

Talent Development

The Discipline of Talent Development was a critical piece of the growth puzzle that we saw across the firms we studied. There was a significant focus on assessment, hiring, coaching, and promoting the internal talent needed to drive organizational growth. Many of the firms we spoke with have been members of both SIA's Fastest-Growing Staffing Firm list and SIA's ranking of the Best Staffing Firms to Work For. We find that the correlation between the two go hand in hand with a high-performance culture. This discipline is especially critical in a service business, like staffing, where growth is highly dependent on ensuring the right people are in the right roles and that those people are well coached on how to do their jobs.

Execution

Staffing firms that break through the barriers to growth do not accomplish it without relentlessly driving execution in their sales force and in their recruiting teams. The Discipline of Execution includes well-defined sales and recruiting practices supported by the right structure and strong leadership. Sales and recruiting are capabilities that require continuous focus and energy from leaders to ensure ongoing competitiveness.

Wrapping Up

There is no status quo for your staffing business. Either grow your business or watch it shrink; standing still is not an option.

While the clear majority of staffing firms will never grow beyond $5 million in revenue, those who want more must be prepared for a challenging journey. This journey begins with you, the leaders of the business. Are you willing to invest and make sacrifices? Are you willing to change? If so, you will benefit from the lessons of others, as we look at how the five Leadership Disciplines allow you to successfully navigate through the challenges of growth while giving you and your team the skills necessary to break through.

BREAKING THROUGH

Chapter 3:
The Discipline of Commitment

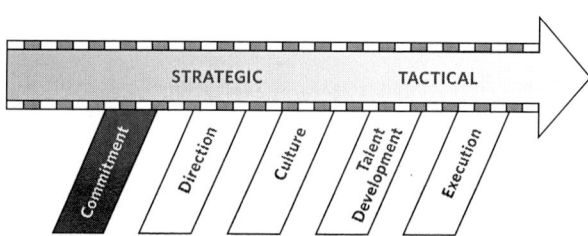

Commitment is one quality above all others that enables a potential leader to become a successful leader. Without commitment, there can be no success.
—John Maxwell[16]

The Discipline of Commitment revealed itself at a roundtable discussion with half a dozen leaders of top-performing staffing firms as they each shared their personal background and their company history. While each of their stories was very different, a common thread existed among them. They all spoke of an unwavering commitment to growing their companies. This commitment to growth drove them to make personal and professional sacrifices, as well as being willing to take risks that most business owners simply would not take. We call this the Discipline of Commitment.

Much of what you will read in this chapter is consistent with the mission, vision, and values framework that has been a pillar of business planning for decades. However, the Discipline of Commitment is more than a business exercise that ends up becoming placards on the wall. Instead, the Discipline of Commitment is intimate and personal, built on the passions and priorities of the founders and embedded in how they lead. These passions and priorities are then embraced by their team, becoming foundational parts of every aspect of the business.

A Tale of Two Leaders

David—Successful Lifestyle Business Owner

David was the CEO and founder of a small, successful IT staffing firm and loved coming into the office every day to catch up with his employees. Four of his employees had been with him for over 10 years, and while he had trouble retaining new employees, he could always count on his "core four." These employees were not top producers, but they made up for it in their tenure and loyalty. In many ways, they were more like a second family than employees.

David was the face of the business. He was the company's best salesperson and always had been. Since the time of the company's formation, every major client could be linked directly to David. While he attempted to hire new salespeople, he could never find one who could do what he did. Training them was tedious, time consuming, and expensive, and thus far had shown little to no return. While he was always on the lookout for his next salesperson, he no longer saw it as a top priority. He was the best salesperson he knew, and he wasn't about to stop selling. He also had Cheryl.

Cheryl was one of his "core four" and was invaluable to David. She loved the details and was passionate about finding new ways to improve the recruiting team through training as well as keeping up with the latest tools. Cheryl's initiative made her an informal leader on the team and helped ensure that the team stayed competitive. Her attention to detail and passion for recruiting made her an ideal complement to David, allowing him to focus on keeping his customers and his team happy.

More importantly, David had a healthy fear of losing his existing clients, based on personal experience. When he was a top salesperson for another company, David received a "Dear John" phone call from his largest client. Due to cutbacks, he lost over 75% of his gross margin within 72 hours. The lesson stuck. He realized that every client is temporary, regardless of how much business they do with you or how much they like you.

This healthy paranoia ensured that David dedicated time to finding new clients. Over time, David landed new clients and buffered his company from inevitable client turnover. David's company was financially healthy with a loyal customer base and solid employees. It had all the advantages of a well-managed lifestyle business, and while the company had experienced growth and contraction over the years, David had the company he wanted.

Tara—Growth-Driven Executive

Now let us turn to the case of Tara. The last eight years were a whirlwind for her and her business. The company she started became almost unrecognizable. The challenges and successes she experienced forced her to change as a leader. She did not start the company believing it would grow to what it is today; all she knew was that she wanted a company of her own and she wanted it to leave a mark.

Tara respected her former employer, and they treated her well. However, over time it became clearer and clearer that she had a different vision of the staffing business, a vision that she became more and more passionate about every day. Eventually, it became clear to her that it was time to leave, and if she did not, she would regret it.

Tara left and started her company right in the middle of the mid-nineties IT boom in Atlanta, at the time one of the hottest markets in the country. Tara quickly landed business and hired an old school recruiter, Travis. There was no question that Travis's salary demands stretched the boundaries of what she could pay. But Tara needed a senior recruiter who knew how to source talent without the benefit of ad responses or a robust database. So she took the leap.

The skills Travis brought to the organization allowed Tara to focus on building a client base. As job order volume increased, new recruiters were brought in and trained by Travis. Tara hired account managers to help service the larger accounts that she simply did not have time to support properly. Hiring these account managers also forced her to invest more in recruiting. With all the growth, it was time for Tara to move into new office space. Tara saw the potential and knew she needed to invest, even if it meant taking less cash out of the business. She invested in office space that would hold a team triple the size of her current employees. This sign of confidence sent a message to everyone in the organization and energized most of the team to work even harder.

Despite this success, problems began to surface, which brought Tara to an important crossroads. While Travis was excellent at sourcing and placing candidates, he had no patience for management. Also, as the company grew and matured, philosophical differences between Travis and Tara became more and more pronounced. These differences had always existed underneath the surface but only now were becoming a problem. Fundamentally, Travis hated structure and fed on recognition. These two attributes may have worked for a producer in a small company, but they became significant liabilities as the company grew. Disagreements reached a peak when Travis wanted an official promotion to the Recruiting Manager role. Even though she felt she owed it to him, she knew this would not work.

Tara did not know what to do. Travis had been with her since the beginning, and she knew she would not be where she was without his contribution. She decided to call Don, a family friend who had successfully started and sold three companies. She spoke to him in depth about the company's situation, and he made three simple points that have guided her decision making ever since:

- Leaders must make decisions in the best interest of the company, even when they are personally difficult.
- The strength of the leadership team will determine how far the company will go.
- Leaders must continuously grow. In growing a company, challenges become more complex, and leaders must prepare themselves accordingly.

The next day, Tara sat down with Travis and let him know that while she very much valued him as a recruiter, in her judgment, he did not have the skills or the motivation to be Recruiting Manager. In addition, they discussed his deteriorating attitude and its impact on the business. While the discussion was difficult and ultimately resulted in her letting Travis go, Tara knew it was the right thing to do.

Tara then immediately began looking for her right-hand leader—someone with management experience, someone she could trust, and someone she could both teach and learn from. Most people thought she had over-hired when she brought Jen on board. Jen was a VP from a much larger staffing firm, but it quickly became clear that Jen brought a level of professionalism and structure the company needed to reach the next level.

As the company continued to grow, Tara knew she would have both personal and professional challenges. In a sense, she felt that she was learning her job every day. For additional support, she formed an advisory board that held her accountable and gave her guidance on how to become a more effective leader. She also made a point of developing close relationships with other staffing executives who shared war stories and kept her from becoming isolated. Growing her company required sacrifice, risk, and dedication, but she was not done yet; even at $100 million, she knew there was more work to be done.

Contrasting David and Tara is not a question of who is right and who is wrong. They are both capable leaders. They are dedicated to their companies and have a strong sense of responsibility to their employees, their customers, and their candidates. They are simply two executives with very different personal priorities and very different perspectives on growth. David wanted the advantages of a lifestyle business: a chance to do work he loved, relatively low risk, incremental change, and a strong core of loyal people. Tara's priorities were very different. She felt compelled to build a company and to grow it. The sacrifices and risks required to get there were not a major part of her calculation.

The personal priorities seen in these two leaders motivate and drive executive behavior and play a pivotal role in determining the type of company they choose to build. Having a strong commitment to growth provides the energy and focus required for a chief executive to take the risk and make the sacrifices necessary to lead their company through radical transformations.

To best understand the Discipline of Commitment, it is critical to understand what fuels it—to answer the question, why grow?

What Is Your Why?

Through the process of researching and writing this book, we have seen that the first ingredient for success is simply the ambition to grow. While there are many different things that fuel ambition, they all inevitably focus on this question: Why? By that we mean, why are you in business, or what is your purpose for the business? The answer to that question varies from founder to founder and is rarely part of a long-term plan. Instead, their Why is a compelling story crafted by a combination of past experiences, current circumstances, and the values they adhere to. The more people we interviewed the more it became clear that the pursuit of growth was a means to an end. That end has a direct line to the question Why?

To clarify the impact on an executive's commitment to growth, we have highlighted four executives' stories. Each story is unique in its own way, but highlights the impact of a compelling Why.

When Mark Eldridge started ALKU, he had a lot to lose, but he had a purpose that overrode the risk. This vision was built largely on a culture that demanded hard work and loyalty but rewarded that with opportunity and the chance to help build a great company. He wanted a company that would reward merit and provide an environment where young professionals could develop both personally and professionally.

For 20 years, I worked at a large staffing firm, and it was not easy to leave. I loved the company, and I loved the people, but I knew if I did not start my company, someday I would regret it. In 2008, I resigned and started ALKU—no investors, no outside help, just me. I had a lot to lose. I had a house as well as the lifestyle I was providing to my wife and kids. A lot was riding on this decision. The easiest thing to do would be to stay in my job, but I knew that for me, it was not an option. I wanted to build and grow a great company. As things started to progress, others were added to the equation and we started to gain some traction.

My experience is that if I focus on what is in it for me and what I am getting, I have already lost why we are in business and what we are trying to do. Instead, I focus on creating an opportunity for all of my employees who are willing to work for it. We have an understanding with every single person that if you do what we ask, work as hard as you possibly can, and have a little smarts, you will be rewarded. That has been the key to our growth.

I do not focus on growing the company; instead, I focus on growing our 135 people and getting them better.

—Mark Eldridge, ALKU

For Mark, a "great company" correlated with maximizing the talents of "great employees." Of course, putting this idea into practice requires a leader focused beyond their own wants and needs, instead focusing on reinforcing a merit-based, competitive culture. Within that culture, his employees matured into reliable professionals, allowing him to build a company that is both financially healthy and personally rewarding.

For Jeff Bowling, founder of The Delta Companies, there was a moment of clarity that defined the purpose of the company and, by default, how he viewed his role. Until that moment, the business had been about maintaining a lifestyle, allowing him to make some money while he was coaching a local baseball team. In August 2003, Jeff brought together the key people in the business and offered them the opportunity to grow the company together.

> When I had the opportunity to buy my investor out, I brought together the top ten or so people in the organization and I said, 'Here is where we are. We don't have the cash to pay you. And we have given away all our receivables to finance the purchase of the business. But, anything we can bill tomorrow I can pay you on.' We had a tear-jerk, gut-check of a meeting and by the end of the meeting people were putting their credit cards in the middle of the table and saying 'Let's go for it.'
>
> Right then in that nanosecond, I understood that not only was this a huge opportunity, but I also had a huge responsibility. Because these people have put their trust in me. From that point on, this was no longer a lifestyle business. Things were done on purpose, planned out, and proactive. And we had to grow to not only meet our company goals, but also the goals of our team members.
>
> —*Jeff Bowling, The Delta Companies*

Jeff realized that the company must provide his people the opportunities and security they deserved for taking a chance on the business. Growth was the only option. In this moment, the business went from a lifestyle business to a business driven by a larger purpose, fundamentally changing how Jeff looked at himself as a leader. Jeff's Why began with his sincere obligation to reward the loyalty his team showed him on that day and has been a driver of the company direction ever since.

For much of my early life, my parents were quite ill and I was the one who had to take care of them. In the late eighties, I made enough money to take care of myself and support my parents, but there was a moment when I had my vision for this business. The reason I started the company is the same vision that drives us every single day. We feel that there are many ways to make money in this business, but if done right, you can also make a difference—not just a difference for our customers but also for our community, particularly in Detroit. That is what drove me to start the company, and I figured if it did not work, I would be where I had been much of my life, which was in debt and out of a job.

—Cindy Pasky, Strategic Staffing Solutions

The story of Cindy Pasky, founder of Strategic Staffing Solutions, provides a different insight on the Why question. While Jeff Bowling experienced a sudden change driven by loyalty and responsibility, Cindy started with a vision of what a staffing company should be if guided by the right values. In addition, because she had to take care of her parents at a young age, she had a resiliency that gave her the confidence not to fear risk. The fact that Cindy pursued her vision is a testament to her confidence, hard work, and perseverance. While there may have been some fear of failure, Cindy knew failure was not fatal. This combination of a vision of what a staffing company should be along with fearlessness generated a commitment that still drives her company today.

Andrew Limouris's Why began with a family promise, a promise that gave him the focus and commitment he needed to build Medix. At the same time, it provided a strong cultural foundation that influenced both who he hired and who he was willing to work with.

The day I opened my doors, my mom and dad were the ones who helped clean my 8x10 office. My mom was a long time janitorial person and my dad was a baker. So my dad carried the boxes up to the office, and my mom decorated it and cleaned it. She made it pretty and made it look organized. Before I walked out of the office, she grabbed me and she said, 'You have my blessing. Everything will go well, just work hard.' Then she went back to Greece. That was the last time she came to the United States.

I was not going to let her down. Regardless of what I might run into, I was going to work through it. There is a term for it, 'the grinders.' These are people who just grind through the challenges that life provides and manage to have the energy to persevere. I look at those first five years and think that our business largely ran on pure emotion. I did not want to let my mom or anyone else down. I remember when I hired one of our first people in 2004. He had left a competitor to come to work for Medix. He shook my hand and asked if this was going to work. I said 'failure is not an option,' and I meant it.

—*Andrew Limouris, Medix*

People take jobs for many reasons. Some people take jobs because of money, others because the commute may be 15 minutes shorter. Many of these employees do a good job, but it is only the employees who embrace committed leadership that help build a legacy. Andrew's commitment to work, along with the culture of service exemplified by the motto "Medix, we got your back" created a hardworking and loyal employee base. While Medix employees may not have met Andrew's mother, they all benefit from the Why she provided him when the company began.

These four stories show that a compelling Why is the driving force behind the Discipline of Commitment, and it begins with the founder. Take a few minutes and think about this in relation to your business. Do you know what your Why is? Do you want to develop and reward young professionals? Do you have a sense of obligation to provide employees career opportunities? Do you want to build a company with a distinct set of values that positively impacts both clients and consultants? Or do you have a financial target to support those closest to you or a legacy you want to build or preserve? Your Why may be different from those we have seen in this chapter, and that is perfectly fine. The key is to have a Why powerful enough to not only motivate you to sacrifice and take risks but also to motivate your team to do the same.

Chapter 3: The Discipline of Commitment

Breaking Through: The Power of Why

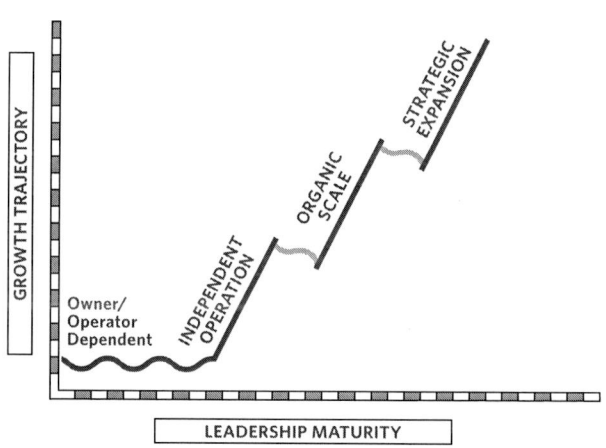

How many of your employees can recite their company's vision and mission statement or the company values? Assuming your employees can recite them, ask yourself, do those statements matter to them? Too often, the answer to the questions above is an emphatic no. Many companies try to address this issue by involving employees in the process of creating the mission, vision, and values. While creating the statements can be a good team building exercise, over time those statements often lose their effectiveness because they are not personally meaningful to employees on a day-to-day basis.

Providing greater meaning begins with a compelling, shared narrative that is embodied by the founder and one that employees can embrace. An effective narrative allows the founder and employees to distinguish themselves from the competition and motivates them to win. This narrative answers the question "Why?" and it defines the shared priorities of both the founder and their employees. In addition, the Power of Why indirectly influences all the other leadership disciplines in very powerful ways. The balance of this chapter will explore both the direct and indirect influences in further detail.

PRIORITIES OF THE LEADER

A powerful Why has a significant psychological impact on the founder, their leadership team, and how they collectively view the purpose of the company. Fundamentally, the Why shifts a founder's thinking from short-term, personal priorities to a long-term legacy.

The most measurable impact is the relationship the executive has with capital. While many founders view company profits through the lens of personal income, executives displaying the Discipline of Commitment prioritize reinvestment into the company. From a financial perspective, it can be said that some founders view their company as an extension of their checkbook, while others view it as an investment. The former tends to be focused on the short-term, while the latter is investing for long-term return. Mark Nussbaum shares their long-term mentality at Signature Consultants.

Early on, and even today, we do not focus on short-term profits, so we can be aggressive about our growth. We have a mindset that is about wanting, thinking, and playing for the long-term, which leads to the willingness to invest versus trading cash. We aren't making decisions based on next week but rather two years from now.

—**Mark Nussbaum, Signature Consultants**

While this perspective certainly covers part of the motivation, it is impossible to ignore the role of legacy building in decision making. For many, it is the desire for a legacy that prioritizes investment over maximizing current income, often superseding short-term financial considerations. This long-term mentality allows the founder to tolerate more risk, recover more quickly from failure, and sacrifice short-term personal wealth to meet the needs of the organization.

Another way founders sacrifice short-term personal priorities is in how they react to the burdens of leading a larger and more complex organization. As companies grow, founders are met with a variety of challenges, many of which are personal in nature. One of the most common challenges is demoting or even terminating friends, partners, or even family members in the best interest of the company. The willingness to make difficult choices that may damage family relationships or friendships is so common that in some ways, it can be considered a rite of passage, differentiating a lifestyle leader from a professional executive.

Sayings such as "It is lonely at the top" and "Heavy is the head that wears the crown" are used to capture the personal sacrifice necessary to be an effective leader. While some may scoff at these sayings as a bit overly dramatic, there is an element of truth in each. The combination of isolation along with greater and greater responsibility is a significant burden of leadership in a firm where commitment is a key discipline. It is one of the reasons why advisory boards and peer groups are so critical in reenergizing and guiding executives, especially as the company progresses through the different phases of growth.

Fundamentally as a company grows, the founder must evolve from a leader of individuals to a leader of teams, and finally, to a leader of leaders. Many of the executives we spoke to highlighted that one of the biggest challenges of growth is that they are constantly relearning their role to keep up with the growing demands of a larger business. This evolution as a leader requires a founder to be willing to reinvent themselves to meet the needs of the company, a discipline that requires humility, work ethic, and patience. For founders who have a compelling Why, evolving as a leader is a reasonable price to pay for the long-term health of the company and the realization of their personal legacy.

Andrew Limouris understands that company growth follows personal growth and that leaders must be willing to make it a priority.

Commitment and grit will only get you so far. Everyone needs to improve, including me. Everybody should have a coach or a mentor. The success we have had at Medix is in large part because our leaders never stop searching for that next coach or mentor and never stop learning. Once you stop learning, you stop innovating and you stop growing. You just kind of stop.

—Andrew Limouris, Medix

Of course, despite attempts at personal growth and learning, there are times when the requirements of leadership are greater than the abilities of the founder. This represents the ultimate crossroads for the founder. Are they willing to give up control for the best interest of the company? Answering yes to that question is a major sacrifice of ego and power, while at the same time, it opens the company to significant risk. However, founders who are committed to growth are also willing to make those sacrifices to secure the company's future, even if that future requires them turning over leadership of the business to someone else.

CREATING SHARED INTEREST

The impact of the Why is not just limited to the priorities of the founder. A strong and compelling purpose creates a shared interest for everyone in the company. When a company's Why is embraced by employees, it fundamentally changes how they view their relationship with the company and their day-to-day work. Employees begin to look beyond their short-term priorities and are willing to make personal sacrifices in the interest of the business. They want to be part of a bigger legacy. They want to build something they could not build on their own and become part of a larger narrative that gives their work greater meaning. Employees know and embrace what makes them better than the competition and what makes the company unique. When their Why is embraced at that level, its impact on behavior and motivation is impossible to overstate.

The Power of Why is not just about creating highly loyal and motivated employees. It also plays an important role in allowing employees to have more purposeful relationships with one another. A strong purpose creates a shared interest that binds employees together. Three simple questions can capture the strength of that bond:

- What do we care about?
- What makes us better than the competition?
- Why do I work here?

The answers to these questions among different employees reflect the effectiveness of the organization's Why. Consistent answers indicate an organization where the purpose significantly influences employee relationships and daily interaction. This influence acts as a reminder of shared beliefs and goals, improving collaboration and conflict resolution. Also, a strong Why strengthens mutual accountability among employees, keeping destructive behavior in check.

In contrast, inconsistency among the answers can reflect weaker team bonds. These weaker bonds allow the short-term interests of employees to play a greater role in defining their peer-to-peer relationships, leaving them more vulnerable to increasing tensions and conflict among employees. This self-centeredness not only undermines collaboration but also requires more management intervention on relatively trivial disagreements. At an extreme, these environments can become fertile grounds for gossip, turf wars, and other destructive behavior.

IMPACT ON OTHER LEADERSHIP DISCIPLINES

The impact of the Why is not limited to just personal priorities and team dynamics. Having a strong purpose and shared mission also impacts all other disciplines that follow it. From the overall company growth strategy to the tactical execution at the producer level, the Power of Why can be found. Below are examples of how an organization's Why can impact the other leadership disciplines beyond Commitment.

Direction

The Discipline of Direction is closely connected to the Why of the company. Direction is about the strategy for the company, including its major goals or purpose. The purpose is often externally focused and defined in terms of service expectations for both clients and consultants. Therefore, the Why heavily influences the creation of company strategy by ensuring that it is consistent with the type of organization the executive wants to build. This includes both selecting the right client base and building the operational capabilities to support them.

Culture

A problem many companies face is ensuring that their culture can withstand the challenges associated with growth. One of the most common challenges is maintaining the culture while daily interaction with the founder becomes more and more limited. The Why provides the catalyst for the transition from a personality-driven culture to a values-driven culture. A values-driven culture allows everyone to become cultural advocates, reducing the dependency on the founder and, thereby, making the culture more resilient and scalable.

Talent Development

The Why's impact on the Discipline of Talent Development falls mainly on the ability to attract and retain talent both from competitors and outside the industry. Organizations with a strong narrative and purpose provide something that is unique in the market and attract talent that can believe in the company's Why. Additionally, having a compelling goal not only attracts talent that identifies with the company's values but also provides a meaningful differentiator, improving employee satisfaction and retention.

Execution

The competitive practices associated with driving sales and recruiting performance are often closely linked to the fulfillment of the founder's Why. Competitive practices, such as how recruiters treat candidates and how sales teams service clients, reflects a particular business philosophy, which is primarily defined by the mission and values of the organization. The links between the Why, the business philosophy, and practices help ensure consistent adoption amongst the team. Also, the links between the Discipline of Execution and the shared purpose of the organization are a key reason it is so difficult to replicate competitive practices from another company.

As organizations grow from Owner/Operator to Independent Operation to Organic Scale, the Discipline of Commitment can change dramatically. In the early years, the challenges are more tactical for many leaders. There are not enough hours in the day, and firefighting takes an increasing amount of time. As the business grows, the challenges become more strategic, involving large investment decisions and complex organizational issues. In addition, the challenge of instilling commitment in a growing company increasingly relies on the company culture. This will be discussed in more detail in Chapter 5.

Wrapping Up

We believe that the Discipline of Commitment is something that is on the border between a discipline and a personality trait. Often, you either have commitment to grow your business or you do not. For those who are not sure they are committed, we encourage some deep introspection to determine what truly motivates you and to what extent you are willing to take risks and make sacrifices to achieve that goal.

Among the leaders of top-performing staffing firms, we found that while each one of them is motivated and highly independent, they also had moments of doubt. Doubt is natural and not necessarily a signal of future failure. The question is not whether your doubt is justified. Instead, the questions that should be asked are whether your Why is powerful enough to overcome your doubts and whether you are able to put solutions in place to address the real challenges that may be at the root of your doubts. Oftentimes doubt is driven by the question "Is growing this company worth all the sacrifices and risks I must take?" Personal sacrifice, financial risk, and an occasional dose of failure are the tolls you may have to pay as a leader of a company committed to growth.

The willingness to pay these tolls is a reflection of your commitment to build something with a purpose. And in many ways, for you as well as the leaders we highlight, building something personally meaningful is the ultimate answer to the question "Why?"

BREAKING THROUGH

Chapter 4:
The Discipline of Direction

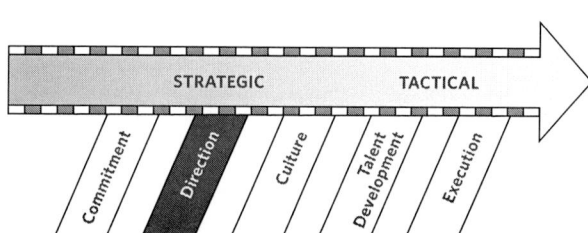

> *All leaders have the capacity to create a compelling vision, one that takes people to a new place, and then to translate that vision into reality.*
> —Warren Bennis[17]

If you walked into a course on strategic planning, you would see analysis around industry trends, competition, opportunities, and threats. The data from this analysis helps establish the direction of the strategy by defining your target market, determining your value proposition, and developing your operational capabilities. Sounds reasonable, but when it comes to the reality of how most staffing companies start, this whole process is largely a work of fiction.

Instead, most founders of staffing companies forgo extensive planning and make a simple leap of faith based on their past experience, personal comfort zone, and gut instinct about what the market needs that they can deliver. This leap-first, plan-later mentality is common in the staffing world. Planning takes time and mental attention that could be better utilized servicing existing clients and finding new ones. This approach works well for most staffing companies for several reasons. First, most founders have their own client base to start the company. There are also very few barriers to entry, including low financial investment. In addition, the marketplace is highly fragmented, indicating that there are more than enough client companies to give the unproven firm a chance. Also, access to much of the talent pool can be obtained for the cost of a job board subscription or for "free" via social media. Fundamentally, staffing is a business tailor made for entrepreneurs, welcoming newcomers to the market every day.

While extensive planning may not take place, most founders have a vision of what they want to create. This vision represents the first step of starting their own business. Typically, the vision is largely a result of a combination of personal and professional beliefs and experiences. As we discussed in the last chapter, it is their Why. For that reason, visions are as varied as the founders who have them.

Regardless of why you started or how you started, if you are committed to growing, it is time to put a competitive strategy in place to set the direction of your company.

This Discipline of Direction focuses on creating a competitive strategy that defines both the target market and the operational model to win market share from the competition. As external market conditions change and/or as the company grows, staffing leaders must actively evaluate where the company is headed to ensure they remain true to their vision and operationally competitive in the fluid world of staffing.

Just as the Discipline of Commitment can be captured by the question "Why?" the Discipline of Direction focuses on the question "What?" What clients will we serve? What is our value proposition? What operational capabilities must we master to compete? What works and does not work regarding our strategy?

The leadership Discipline of Direction addresses these questions and is comprised of three parts. First is developing a well-defined competitive strategy. Second is defining and developing the capabilities needed to execute that strategy. Finally, leaders need to retain strategic foresight to constantly assess and adapt their strategy to threats and opportunities that evolve as the company grows and the competitive landscape changes.

Competitive Strategy

*Efforts and courage are not enough without
purpose and direction.
—John F. Kennedy*[18]

As you look at the external forces facing your staffing business that were discussed in Chapter 1, it is critical to develop and refine your competitive strategy. Choosing the right strategy is as important as how well you execute and operate your business. Great execution cannot make up for a poorly conceived strategy, and choosing the right strategy and market focus can cover for many flaws in execution and business operations.

Dan Campbell of Hire Dynamics notes one piece of advice from a mentor that he will always remember was to "never underestimate the power of a good tailwind." In other words, choose a strategy within an expanding market. Conversely, growing a company is much tougher in a market that is stagnant or declining. The good news is that the staffing industry historically has been an industry with a pretty good tailwind. Just ask executives who find themselves in declining industries, like newspaper publishing, where holding revenue constant from year to year is considered a small victory.

The topic of strategy is often misunderstood and, in many ways, made to seem overly complex. In fact, the best strategies are quite simple and should be easy for leaders and employees to articulate. If you cannot succinctly state your competitive strategy, you are not alone. For many, the competitive choices and strategy they follow are like the air they breathe. It is not readily apparent, but nonetheless, the strategy influences all aspects of your company.

So what is a competitive strategy? There have been many books written on just that subject, but for this exercise, this is the definition we like best for its simplicity: *Competitive strategy is the customers a business chooses to serve and how that business differentiates itself from its competitors and substitutes.*

WHAT CLIENTS WILL YOU SERVE?

The first step in competitive strategy is defining your target market by identifying client characteristics that will provide your sales and marketing team's greater focus. This focus allows sales and marketing efforts to become more scalable since selling to accounts with similar characteristics is more likely to have comparable success factors. For example, selling to local small and medium-sized businesses (SMB) requires a very different approach than developing relationships with Managed Service Providers (MSPs). SMB success factors require a high level of activity with a wide variety of accounts, while MSP driven strategies focus on developing long-term relationships with key decision makers. Not only are these desks managed very differently, but the skills of the personnel must be very different as well.

While it is important to be clear about the customers you will serve, it is equally important to be clear about the customers you will not serve or, at a minimum, you will not proactively sell to. Only by defining your target customers will your team be ready to say no when the opportunity is not a fit and say yes when the right opportunity strikes. In doing so, staffing firms provide clarity to their sales organization and can more rapidly build scalable operational expertise than competitors with a poorly defined market strategy.

Figure 4.1 captures the most common ways target markets are defined in staffing.

WHAT TYPES OF CUSTOMERS WILL YOU SERVE?

Figure 4.1

SEGMENT TYPE	DESCRIPTION
Geography	Which geography will you specialize in—local, regional, national, global, or something else?
Industry	Which industry will you specialize in—government, healthcare, manufacturing, or energy, for example? Or will you work in any industry available?
Skill Type	Which skills will you work on? This is the most common way staffing firms differentiate themselves.
Type of Service	Which services will you provide on your own or with a partnership? (See Figure 1.5: Workforce Solutions Ecosystem) In addition to staffing, many firms also provide some services from other areas of the ecosystem. The most common is process outsourcing or "solutions" work.

WHAT IS YOUR VALUE PROPOSITION?

Once you have defined your target customer, the next question to answer is, "How will you differentiate your business?" At its most basic level, the two main forms of differentiation are low-cost or product/service differentiation. While there are many ways to differentiate a business, one of our favorite frameworks comes from Michael Treacy and Fred Wiersema in their management classic *The Discipline of Market Leaders: Choose Your Customers, Narrow Your Focus, Dominate Your Market.*[19] In this book, the pair lay out three distinct approaches to differentiation.

The three approaches described by Treacy and Wiersema are operational excellence, product leadership, and customer intimacy. Operational excellence focuses on creating a competitive advantage through efficiency. This efficiency allows organizations to service a large client base at highly competitive prices. Walmart is often highlighted as an example of this model. Product leadership focuses on innovation as the primary differentiator. This innovation allows businesses who are product leaders to create compelling products ahead of the competition. These products often have a higher cost/price point. Apple is an excellent example of this model. Customer intimacy leverages higher service levels as their differentiator. These companies are also often at a higher price point but may or may not have high levels of innovation. Ritz-Carlton or other high-level hotels are examples of this approach. Many staffing firms find a customer intimacy approach as a natural strategic fit for their business style, though there are staffing firms using an operational excellence or product leadership approach as well.

These approaches are more than just an occasional choice or decision, but rather a consistent, rigorously practiced and enforced code of conduct or behavior. It is important to note that Treacy and Wiersema maintain that market leaders must choose only one of the approaches to be the best in the business. Those companies that do not have that focus usually suffer from a constant state of muddled compromise and do not become market leaders.

Another effective way to compare competitive strategies in staffing is by understanding the nature of the services they provide and how they are structured operationally to provide them. From VMS focused staffing companies to Statement of Work (SOW) deliverable based companies, each one of them has a distinct sales strategy along with operational and cultural elements that must be aligned.

DEFINE YOUR COMPETITIVE STRATEGY

Figure 4.2

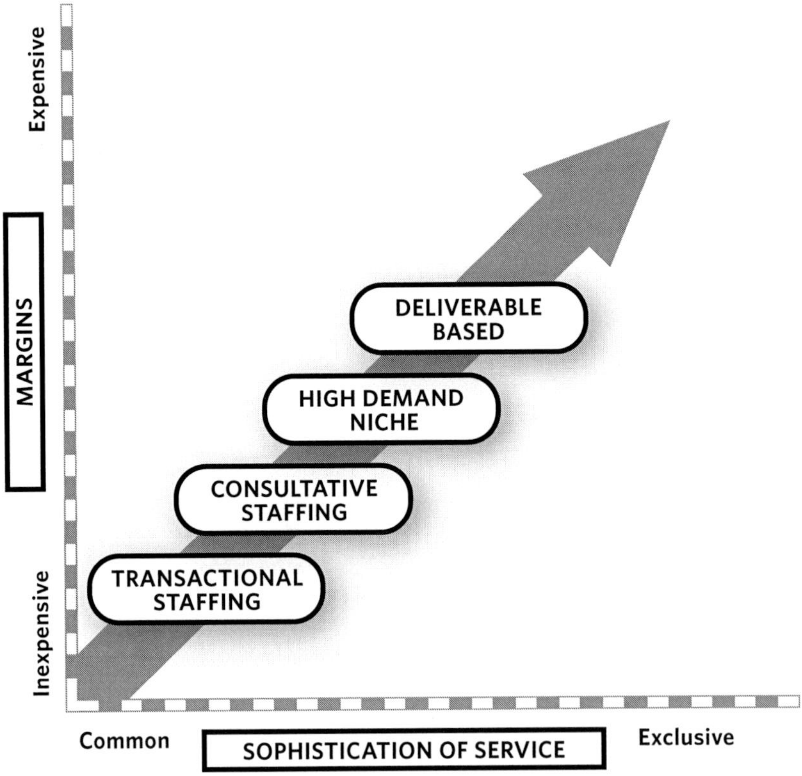

Four competitive strategies are highlighted in Figure 4.2. On the chart, the x-axis captures the sophistication of the service, while the y-axis represents the relative margin of the offering. Next, we will use the strategies to compare operational models and, by doing so, highlight how you should define operational capabilities as part of a greater strategy to build a competitive advantage.

Defining Your Operational Capabilities

The best way to understand a staffing company's strategy is not by reading the business planning document, talking to employees, or even speaking to the chief executive. Instead, a company's strategy is best captured by understanding the type of clients they are targeting and the job orders they decide to work. The day-to-day operations are the only true reflection of the company's current market strategy. For this reason, we will drill down into different competitive strategies in terms of the operational models that support them.

A **Transactional Staffing** model relies on operational efficiency as a competitive advantage. Efficiency enables organizations to generate a large volume of candidates quickly and relatively cheaply. Transactional staffing models are typically seen in lower-end skills or with companies that need to compete in VMS programs that rely heavily on automation and seek to minimize the impact of relationships.

Consultative Staffing companies rely on customer intimacy and quality service as their competitive advantage. While speed is always a factor, the relationship they have with clients and consultants gives them more influence over the hiring process. This influence increases the accuracy of requirements while improving time to hire and quality of fit for the client. Consultative staffing companies often rely on local branch operations to help develop deeper relationships with the customer and consultant base.

A **High Demand Niche** model also focuses on quality and service but is supplemented by specializing in high demand, difficult-to-find skill sets. Often the specialization requires the staffing company to work with clients and consultants from across the country, lending itself to a more centralized model. Sales and recruiting teams support this specialization with an in-depth understanding of the skill set niche and must use more traditional recruiting methods, such as networking and referrals.

A **Deliverable Based** staffing firm may or may not have local offices but requires subject matter experts to both sell and deliver the service. These companies straddle the line between staffing and consulting services and are typically referred to as providing solutions or SOW consulting. They are often just as comfortable being paid on a deliverable basis as they are with a more typical staffing time and material basis. The higher cost of sales and delivery typically requires higher margins. Their ability to provide deliverables allows them to be more creative in the services for their clients.

Operational capabilities represent distinct choices leadership must make, including company culture, organizational structure, hiring profiles, policy changes, process improvements, and new tools. All these decisions are qualified with the question "How does this change allow us to execute our competitive strategy more effectively?" The Discipline of Execution will be explored more thoroughly in Chapter 7.

Top-performing staffing executives use this focus to craft an intimate bond between their target market and their operations, thus creating a competitive advantage that is both scalable and agile. In contrast, organizations that attempt to support more than one competitive strategy are, in effect, trying to run multiple operations concurrently. For smaller staffing companies, this can quickly reduce competitiveness by both causing confusion with clients and employees, and straining the company's limited financial and personnel resources.

The most common example of this, which we often see, is when consultative staffing firms with a branch structure attempt to bring on more transactional staffing business, often through supporting large staffing programs. These organizations begin supporting this business through their branches, and inevitably, the conflict between the two models begins to stress the branch, causing production to decrease. Eventually, if the volume of business justifies it, the firm may pull the VMS business from the branch and create a dedicated operation focusing solely on the transactional business. Now the company must support two operations that require different cultures, personnel, processes, and tools. The company is now split between two separate competitive strategies that distract the executive team and divide monetary resources, which can impair growth and reduce the odds of success.

Strategic Foresight

To break through these barriers to growth, leaders must balance the tactical with the strategic and not let the day-to-day dominate their time and thinking. Eventually, they must pull themselves out of "working in" the business and begin "working on" the business to foresee the potential opportunities and threats the business is facing. That is the essence of strategic foresight, which requires two things. First, leaders must be able to retain an external perspective on the business. Second, they must understand the financial state of the business and make appropriate financial decisions.

It is easy for executives to get lost in the details of the daily operations. However, as a company grows, executives must find a balance between managing internal issues and understanding what is happening with their clients and the market as a whole. Sales focused executives have an advantage in this area since they naturally desire interaction with clients. This interaction provides them important firsthand awareness of the challenges their clients are facing. This perspective allows them to modify their strategy based on the opportunities and threats presented to them.

In addition, being externally focused requires getting different perspectives from other professionals in the industry. This perspective can be obtained in a variety of ways, including networking with other executives, establishing an advisory board, and participating in associations and conferences.

One of the most important factors in strategic foresight is the ability to strengthen a firm's competitive position by funding growth while remaining financially strong. It is important to note that what is written here is not meant to be financial advice. Instead, we are attempting merely to highlight the role managing capital has in a growing organization.

Undercapitalization is a common and significant obstacle to growth. A chief executive can have great people, great operations, and an excellent strategy. However, the ability to fund growth is a factor that if not properly managed, can stop growth in its tracks or at least make the cost of growth much more expensive.

There are many institutions that are willing to provide cash to fund payroll and internal investments as well as acquisitions. However, the amount and the purpose of the funding can significantly impact both the terms of the funding and flexibility moving forward.

One of the most common types of loans are lines of credit provided by banks. These are revolving loans that are meant to supply cash for short-term needs. In staffing, the need for a short-term loan is driven primarily by the growth of contractor payroll. They are not intended to provide funding for operational investments. However, they do indirectly free up cash to provide flexibility for firms to reinvest in the business.

If the business does not have the option for a line of credit, then factoring or payroll funding is a natural choice. Unlike a line of credit, which acts more like a credit card of the business, a factoring or payroll funding company uses the receivables as collateral for the loan. Therefore, the bigger the receivables the more money can be used to fund payroll. There are also companies that provide these financing services and specialize primarily in serving the staffing industry. Many of these provide a range of additional services, including back-office support, invoicing, or payroll processing, or even act as employer of record for the temporary workers.

A common mistake owners make is to support unprofitable operations through their short-term funding. This misuse of funding can be very tempting, but it is not sustainable. When a company is unprofitable, it drains its cash reserves, and as capital becomes more and more depleted, the company must rely more and more on outside funding to meet external payroll obligations. This is fine if the company eventually grows or cuts costs to become profitable. However, if nothing changes, then either the line of credit will reach its limit or the receivables will not be enough to factor payroll. In those cases, the owner is unable to fund payroll, a scenario that can ruin the company's reputation and can quickly bring them to the brink of insolvency.

So how does a chief executive who has no financial background develop the skill and knowledge necessary to ensure the monetary health of a more and more complex organization? While it is important for chief executives to educate themselves as much as possible, eventually they need to hire financial professionals they can trust, including a chief financial officer (CFO).

CONTROLLER VS CFO RESPONSIBILITIES

Figure 4.3

Controller Responsibilities	CFO Responsibilities
Payroll	Investment Analysis
Accounts Receivable	Financial Forecasting
Accounts Payable	Manage Banking Relationships
General Ledger	Evaluate Loan Conditions
Financial Statements	Trusted Business Advisor to Owner
Budgeting	Primary Liaison with Accountant
Tax Compliance	Provide Strategic Analysis from Financial Reporting
Cost Accounting	Make Recommendations on Cost Improvements

In a company's early phases, it may simply need a controller to manage the back office. However, too often, companies make the mistake of thinking their controller is a CFO. The cost of this mistake can be minimal up to the Independent Operation phase. However, as a company continues to grow, financial decisions become more complicated and strategic. The controller can become overwhelmed, and the company is vulnerable to overpaying for capital or making poor investment decisions. Figure 4.3 contrasts the operational role of the controller with the more strategic role of the CFO.

As seen in Figure 4.3, the controller's primary job is to manage the day-to-day back-office operations. In contrast, the CFO acts as a close advisor to the chief executive, providing business insight from a financial professional's perspective. Ideally, the CFO should evolve and become more strategic as the company grows. The relationship between the CFO and the chief executive ideally is that of a strategic partner who can have in-depth, substantive discussion on the financial state of the business. These discussions can lead to conflict between the two, but through that conflict, the chief executive receives a more complete picture of the health of the company and the CFO understands the other external concerns the company is facing. This transparency and collaboration leads to stronger decision making for the long-term.

The leadership Discipline of Direction answers the question "What do I want this organization to become?" Answering this question includes defining the clients you choose to support, the operational capabilities to support it, and the foresight to make crucial strategic decisions. However, the direction you choose is built on a set of assumptions that may no longer apply due to changing conditions both in the marketplace and internally. This requires that you build both a focused and an adaptable organization. The next section will discuss how assessing and adapting play an important role in ensuring the company is heading in the right direction to break through the different phases of growth.

Breaking Through: Assess and Adapt

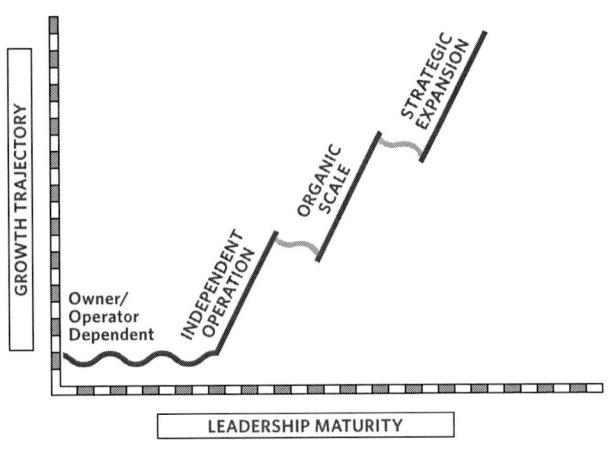

Chapter 4: The Discipline of Direction

Every success story is a tale of constant
adaptation, revision, and change.
—Richard Branson[20]

It is important to keep in mind that any strategy is built on a set of assumptions. We often assume the market is going to remain healthy, our sales strategies are going to engage buyers effectively, and how we deliver our service is consistent with the needs of the client. This Discipline of Direction must evolve and mature as an organization moves through the different phases of growth and does so by being able to accurately assess the current direction and adapt accordingly. Assessing and adapting are not about knee-jerk reactions to events but instead are about well thought out challenges to our assumptions about the state of the strategy by analyzing observable patterns.

When a company is in the Owner/Operator phase, assessing and adapting are simple. The Owner/Operator has visibility into the market and day-to-day operations as well as the financials. In addition, if the organization needs to modify its course, the team is small enough that they can adapt relatively quickly. However, once the Owner/Operator decides they want to grow, assessing and adapting become more difficult due to greater complexity and lower visibility.

Understanding how to assess and adapt the strategy as the company grows is a significant challenge for staffing executives. The remainder of this chapter will discuss how the leadership Discipline of Direction must evolve as the company transitions through the different phases of growth. We will refer to examples from top-performing staffing executives to explain how they had to evolve both themselves and their leadership teams to ensure their organizations continued in the right direction.

BUILDING AN INDEPENDENT OPERATION

At the most fundamental level, breaking through the Owner/Operator phase is about creating a largely Independent Operation that no longer depends on the founders to drive daily transactions. Instead of participating in the daily blocking and tackling of the business, the founders can now dedicate a good portion of their focus on longer-term growth obstacles and opportunities.

One of the first steps in achieving self-sufficiency is a strategy that can be understood and adhered to by the entire team. This means knowing what niche they serve, who their clients are, and how they work together in order to become successful. This also means saying no to business that does not fit within the strategy. The go/no-go decision is an early indicator of the Discipline of Direction. It is also one of the most difficult thresholds executives must cross on their path to building an Independent Operation.

In Mark Eldridge's business, you can see how the Owner/Operator phase at ALKU acted as the testing ground for defining his competitive strategy. While some executives have a competitive strategy in mind when they start a company, it is very common for the competitive strategy to be clarified by the interaction with companies and candidates in the marketplace.

I formed ALKU in 2008, a few months before the financial crisis. The initial vision for the company was to build an IT staffing company. Then the financial crisis hit in the fall of 2008, and it hit the market like a tsunami. Despite that, we continued to make calls and work any legitimate opening we could find. By March of 2009, we had survived many failures, but the successes we had were pointing to a compelling direction.

Chapter 4: The Discipline of Direction

The financial crisis forced companies to reduce their personnel to save on costs. For large companies running Enterprise Resource Planning (ERP) systems, one of the most effective ways to do that was to add functionality to their current software. To capitalize on that insight, by April of 2009, we shifted our direction to focus solely on ERP. That meant that instead of saying yes to every IT job that came in, we had to start saying no.

It took probably another three months before we realized that we had the discipline to execute that focus. It was in 2009. I remember we'd done a really good job for a client down in Texas. The client said, 'You could fill PeopleSoft jobs faster than anybody I have ever worked with. Can you help me with these dot net positions?' We thought about it a minute and ultimately said, 'No, that is not what we do.' We hung up that phone, and the three of us looked at each other and were scared out of our minds. Did we just make a mistake? We left work that evening saying to each other, 'If we need to, we can call him back tomorrow and tell him we can help with those jobs after all. Let's just think about it tonight, and let's try to fill some more PeopleSoft jobs.'

And then I don't know if it was fate, but we came into work in the morning and all these other things that we were working on, specifically in the world of ERP, started to take off. We were busy and not sitting around wondering what to do with our time. Ever since then, we've been focused on ERP and realized that NO was one of the most powerful lessons we could learn about strategy.

—Mark Eldridge, ALKU

While all Owner/Operators have access to the same information, top-performing executives use that information to refine their approach to their market strategy. Mark's story highlights how an executive can take market feedback, assess their current positioning, and make critical strategic decisions. This feedback does not remove all doubt but can provide a clearer path. If the executive remains engaged, they have the visibility they need to assess and adapt. Over time, additional feedback may require the executive to modify the path they have chosen, but there is a path nonetheless.

Adaptation helps define not only market strategy but also how operations need to change in the future. A clear direction includes providing the operational vision and alignment between strategy and execution. In ALKU's case, this alignment required a painful decision to say no based on the principle that regardless of the stated strategy, staffing executives must understand that the direction of the company is driven primarily by the clients they choose and the job orders they work.

Mark's ability and decision to refine his competitive strategy required discipline, but it also provided clarity. He now knew who his salespeople needed to call, what talent they had to recruit, and how they needed to act every day to be successful. Standard policies, processes, and tools enabled turn-key operations to be developed. More importantly, he provided clarity to his leadership team on what is required of them to grow the business. This clarity aligns the leadership team, empowering them to lead with little tactical oversight from the chief executive, and thus provides the foundation for Organic Scale.

From a financial perspective, the Owner/Operator's ability to move from a consumer of company profits to an investor in the company is a crucial transition. The ability to retain earnings in the organization allows for investment, but it also establishes the leadership team as a responsible steward of financial resources for future lenders.

ACHIEVING ORGANIC SCALE

The Organic Scale phase is about building the capability to replicate an Independent Operation to capture greater market share. Some companies may choose to open more remote branches, while others may choose a more centralized approach. Regardless of how the organization grows, the leadership Discipline of Direction becomes more difficult, primarily due to three challenges in the Organic Scale phase:

1. Increased Complexity of Execution
2. Lack of Direct Observation
3. Inability to Influence

Increased Complexity of Execution: Executives can no longer drive the strategy on their own. Instead, they need leaders who are passionate about the strategy and will actively execute it. In top-performing organizations, this oftentimes is made up of original team members who were there from the early days of the company.

Lack of Direct Observation: In larger organizations, the executive can no longer rely on direct observation to identify patterns in operations or their competitive strategy. Without additional sources of information, they make decisions from partial and often inaccurate information. Poorly informed executives tend to become less and less effective as the organization grows, rolling out solutions that are unsuccessful and, in some cases, making the problem worse or creating new ones.

Inability to Influence: Adapting a larger organization is more difficult and requires a concerted effort from all the leaders in the organization. In most cases, adapting is about changing behavior at a desk level. As a company grows, the executive does not have the bandwidth to drive behavior at each individual desk. To influence employee behavior, executives must rely on other leaders to drive buy-in and adoption. This delegation of leadership is a critical step to ensuring an organization stays focused and aligned to the strategy.

To address these challenges, the chief executive must first strengthen the internal advocacy of the strategy, delegate decision making, and build a management system that provides important data. The most important, and often most difficult, of these is delegating decision making.

For many of the top-performing executives, releasing control is a difficult but crucial step for them to make as a leader. Take the case of Ron Shahani at Acro Service Corporation.

When we were approaching $10 million, I realized that if we were going to continue to grow, we needed greater clarity and buy-in from the team. It could not just be my vision anymore. I needed them to own the vision as well. From that point on, I made sure that I involved key members of the team in developing our strategic objectives. In the end, they executed the vision, so they needed to be empowered and trained to execute it.

—Ron Shahani, Acro Service Corporation

In Ron's case, he understood that the team lacked alignment and accountability. His approach to rectify that was to involve principle members in developing the company strategic objectives at around the $10 million mark. This collaborative approach not only allowed his leaders to have greater buy-in but also educated them on the assumptions and business rationale behind the competitive strategy. This knowledge empowers leaders to more effectively assess and adapt their own operations to meet the unique needs of their markets. It also allows local leaders to develop strategic problem solving skills that are beneficial not only for addressing current obstacles but also in taking on more responsibility as the organization grows.

There are many ways to increase strategic problem solving skills among the leadership team, including one-on-one coaching and formal workshops. Workshops are a particularly effective approach for leaders with a more collaborative leadership style. In addition, this approach becomes more powerful when companies are reaching the $10 to $15 million range.

Strategy workshops can also help identify weaknesses within the management team that need to be addressed. Some of these weaknesses are simply based on a lack of knowledge or experience, while others are deeper and more complex to address, such as a lack of buy-in on the strategy or a lack of overall trust for the chief executive and among the leadership team.

Holding leaders accountable is another key success factor of Organic Scale. This is especially true for leaders in remote branches.

Going from a single branch to Organic Scale was when we really started measuring our gross profit per person on a weekly basis and using that as a metric around efficiency. We wanted to keep our measures as simple as possible so we could build in standards and systems without being micromanagers. This approach empowered the branch managers to decide when they hired, but it was based on the metrics. They all knew what numbers they needed to hit; there was no gray area. That was a really big one for us.

—Dan Campbell, Hire Dynamics

Dan's story illustrates two of the key requirements for effective direction in the Organic Scale phase. First, he developed a management system that provided consistent guidelines for management decision making. Second, he used that management system as a framework for effective delegation.

Management systems bolstered by well-defined performance metrics allow the chief executive to take a "trust but verify" approach with their leaders. These simple guidelines worked for Dan's management style and the culture of Hire Dynamics. Some leaders may require more robust metrics to feel comfortable in delegating authority to their teams, but Dan's approach touches on what we believe is a fundamental truth when it comes to metrics: *When using metrics as a tool to manage your employees, keep them as simple as possible.*

The system put in place at Hire Dynamics gave Dan the confidence to delegate decision making to his leaders. This delegation strengthens direction by allowing leaders to truly own the execution of the strategy for their market. That ownership not only acts as a platform for their development as leaders, but it also ensures clear accountability for the decisions that they make. These managers have the authority, and will eventually develop the skills, to act as the eyes and ears for their markets, thus scaling strategic foresight.

In addition, as branches are added, management relies more and more on metrics as an important tool to evaluate the health of the business and collaborate on solutions. The bigger the organization the more important data-based decision making becomes. With the right metrics in place, the management team now has the language necessary to assess the progress of the strategy as well as work together to identify root causes of non-performance. This structure and improved management collaboration allows more offices to be opened successfully, thus enabling a key success factor of Organic Scale. In addition, metrics provide the foundation for more effective company-wide communication, allowing the chief executive to keep the team updated on the progress of the company based on measurable goals. This helps keep employees informed and allows them to feel connected to the overall direction and success of the company.

Organic Scale presents significant financial challenges that require greater focus and expertise. The first challenge is the high level of capital investment required to open new operations. Instead of just scaling production head count, the chief executive must now invest in office space and line-level leadership in markets where they have minimum, if any, market share. The combination of increased costs along with immature markets can quickly turn new branches into substantial money pits. In addition, the increased complexity of the operations requires more sophisticated analysis and forecasting. To overcome these challenges, the CFO should now be a key member of the executive team, providing financial analysis, strategic insight, and leadership around complicated relationships with vendors, such as tax accountants and financial partners.

As an organization achieves Organic Scale, the chief executive must both strengthen their own ability to provide direction and develop the same focus within their leadership team. Through effective delegation and communication, successful organizations can achieve both.

EXPANDING YOUR STRATEGY

The Strategic Expansion phase focuses on growth through acquisition or the development of new competitive strategies to supplement or replace Organic Scale as the primary driver of growth. Staffing executives choose Strategic Expansion as a growth strategy for a variety of reasons. There are times when expansion is part of a long-term plan and other times when it can be opportunistic. Regardless of the timing, we believe there are two important considerations relative to Strategic Expansion and the Discipline of Direction: adequate financial resources and compatibility between the legacy strategy and the new strategy.

Strategic Expansion poses significant financial challenges that must be considered. Whether it is a decision to acquire another company or just organically expand service offerings, the ability to assess the financial strain of Strategic Expansion should not be underestimated. Some organizations save up enough retained earnings for expansion. In those cases, the CFO must be able to forecast the financial investment and closely monitor the ongoing impact of the new strategy.

If Strategic Expansion requires outside capital, then "angel investors" or private equity firms may need to be engaged. The CFO must not only be able to collaborate with those investors, but they must also be able to provide insight to the executive on the pluses and minuses of the options presented to them. In addition, the CFO becomes a key contact for those investors, providing them the reporting and other financial information they need to remain informed about their investment.

> *Most successful companies achieve most of their growth by expanding into logical adjacencies that have shared economics and reinforce the core business, not from unrelated diversification or moves into "hot" markets.*
> —Chris Zook and James Allen[21]

Because of the strain on capital associated with Strategic Expansion, it poses significant risk. To increase the likelihood of success while reducing risk, Chris Zook and James Allen wrote *Profit from the Core*. When considering Strategic Expansion, it is useful to consider the following prescription from the book.

Chris Zook and James Allen ask executives to find a business that is closely related to the core business and to look for compatibility between the two strategies. Regardless of how and why executives choose to grow via Strategic Expansion, an important consideration is how closely aligned the new strategy is to the existing strategy of the company.

As we discussed earlier, the Discipline of Direction requires leaders to accomplish three major things. These include defining your competitive strategy, building your operational capabilities required to serve it, and retaining your strategic foresight. Strategies that have similarities will also have compatibilities with the existing direction, allowing you to leverage those similarities for competitive advantage. If you decide to take on new strategy that has no compatibility in terms of clients, operational capabilities, or foresight, then the risks associated increase substantially. An example of the impact of compatibilities in both client and business operations is highlighted by Jeff Bowling of The Delta Companies.

We were doing only physician direct hire (100% retained) in 2003. In 2004, we brought in a sales leader, Sherri Carlton, with deep Locum Tenens experience to start that specialty. We did not have a lot of crossover, but she was able to use our good name and reputation in the marketplace to get orders and candidates. We have always done a great job taking care of customers, and we were able to really capitalize on that when we started Locum Tenens.

We ended up more concentrated in rural America in our Locum Tenens business than most other firms since that was largely where our physician retained business was located. The customer demographic has changed over the years, but that is how we got started leveraging our existing strength with clients.

—Jeff Bowling, The Delta Companies

In this example, Delta's expansion to Locum Tenens illustrates how leveraging compatibilities between strategies provides a significant competitive advantage. Even though this expansion occurred early in the company formation, it illustrates the importance of adjacencies when considering Strategic Expansion. To explore the advantages of adjacencies further, we will look at Delta's example from an external and an internal perspective.

Strategies that have similar compatibilities in the customers they target have significant advantages. The most direct advantage is simply the ability to infuse the new service offering into existing accounts or related companies. Leveraging an existing account base can provide a strong foundation for a new service offering. While there was not a lot of direct crossover, Delta's reputation in the healthcare markets opened doors for the new division.

There are risks in leveraging the current account base to support a new division. The biggest risk is the impact failure can have on the reputation of current accounts. Delta addressed the risk by hiring an experienced practitioner to run the new division.

The other common risk is client confusion. Clients view your company through the lens of your value proposition. Expanding into new competitive strategies can cause client confusion if the value propositions are significantly different. In this case, the two niches focused on providing physicians to rural areas. The only difference is whether the physician was placed in a contract or a permanent role, thus minimizing the risk of confusion.

Internal Perspective

From a delivery perspective, recruiters struggle to support different customers that require them to adjust how they run their desk. The most common example of this is trying to have a consultative recruiter support transactional VMS business. Jeff noted that the current recruiting methodologies were very compatible and considered that a competitive advantage.

In addition, when a new offering can leverage the current candidate pool, recruiters have a much lower learning curve and can potentially use their existing networks. These compatibilities allow the new offering to scale much more quickly, especially for offerings that rely on difficult-to-find talent. In Delta's case with Locum Tenens, the only difference in the talent pool is whether the doctor is interested in contract or permanent positions.

Another internal consideration is the ability to effectively scale both sales and recruiting. If you have an offering that requires different skills, it adds significant complexity to ramping up producers. In this case, a Locums Tenens leader was brought in to fill the gaps on the sales side, while the recruiters could apply many skills they learned, supporting the core offering.

We believe that Delta's transition to Locum Tenens had strong compatibilities. That ability to leverage both the compatibilities and the hiring of a sales practitioner was one of the key decisions that allowed the company to grow almost 60% a year for five years, reaching $55 million by 2008.

While it can be enormously successful, as Delta proved, we should note that Strategic Expansion is not always the answer to growth if the compatibilities cannot be properly leveraged. Another quote from *Profit from the Core* makes this observation:

> *Building unique strength in a core business, no matter how small or narrowly focused, is the key to subsequent growth. Many companies that neglect this principle retrench and return to the core. In fact, sometimes the right strategy is to even "shrink to grow," going back to the core.*
> —Chris Zook and James Allen[22]

One executive who took that advice was Dan Campbell at Hire Dynamics, who at one time was trying to support multiple staffing verticals. Dan, with help from his board, determined that he needed to "shrink to grow."

> *We found ourselves at a point where I think one of our biggest mistakes was diverting from what we were really great at and not just sticking to our knitting in commercial staffing. We were at $40 million in revenue and woke up in 2007/2008 with four divisions doing everything from pharmacy staffing to finance and accounting to sales and executive search. That is where having a board really counts, as they said to us, 'You are good, but if you are ever going to be great, you have got to focus.' And we did.*
>
> *While everyone else was going upstream, we went the other way and sold our pharmacy staffing. Even though we started in big four accounting firms, we had to admit that we were not good in finance and accounting. Once we focused, that was when our growth really took off.*
>
> —Dan Campbell, Hire Dynamics

The leadership Discipline of Direction becomes substantially more complicated when attempting to maneuver the company through multiple strategies. When considering Strategic Expansion, advice from other high-level executives becomes even more crucial due to the amount of risk and investment. Advisory boards or boards of directors can provide impartial advice and ask important questions that the chief executive might overlook. Many of the executives we spoke with had, at one point or another, either created an advisory board or found more informal outside mentors to aid them in strategic decision making. An advisory board need not have any formal role beyond providing advice for the chief executive while still allowing the executive/owner to retain control.

Some executives have such a high level of confidence in their leadership team that they are reluctant to look to the outside for advice. However, regardless of how strong the team is, there is a tendency for leaders to share the same biases and blind spots. In addition, internal leaders may have other motivations to pursue or reject a new strategy that is not in the company's best interest. An advisory board addresses these issues by creating a team of peers whose primary function is to challenge the chief executive and provide advice from an external perspective. Ideally, an advisory board would be comprised of professionals who have relatively diverse business experience in various industries. The perspective of the board can then be balanced with the perspective of the internal leaders, leading to more dynamic and productive vetting of new strategies.

Strategic Expansion adds multiple factors that are both internal and external in nature, many of which the chief executive may have no previous experience with. For this reason, chief executives must be selective in choosing their strategies and ensuring they have the talent with the necessary subject matter expertise to assess and adapt the organization. The right strategy and the right people will substantially reduce risk while maximizing the return on Strategic Expansion.

Wrapping Up

As organizations break through from one phase to another, the leadership Discipline of Direction must keep the company focused while, at the same time, adapting to changing conditions. The ability to assess and adapt requires both market knowledge and awareness of the relative strengths and weaknesses of the operations. As the organization grows, this knowledge is transferred from executive management to line-level leaders. This transfer requires line-level leaders to develop strategic problem solving skills to ensure their operations are adapting to meet the unique needs of their market. From the perspective of Strategic Expansion, the Discipline of Direction requires leaders to understand how compatible new growth strategies are and understand the financial and operational impact adopting a new strategy can have on an organization.

SUCCESS FACTORS FOR BREAKING THROUGH THE DISCIPLINE OF DIRECTION

Figure 4.4

Phases	Direction
Building an Independent Operation	Refine the competitive strategy using feedback from clients to better identify the target market as well as more clearly define the needed operational capabilities.
Achieving Organic Scale	Identify and develop leaders either externally or internally. Develop a management system establishing KPIs for individual operations. Have frequent management meetings to drive top-down and bottom-up communication.
Expanding Your Strategy	Chief executive commits to a peer networking group or board to provide business advisory and improve accountability. Hire outside expertise to address experience gaps. Understand how compatible strategies are to one another and ensure the financial and operational impacts of the new strategy are well understood.

BREAKING THROUGH

Chapter 5:
The Discipline of Culture

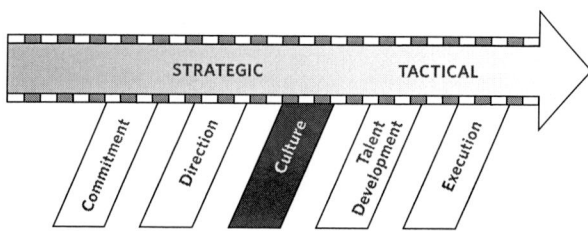

Culture Eats Strategy for Breakfast[23]

Staffing is a people business. It requires teams with different backgrounds and experience levels to engage in conflict as well as motivate one another to a common goal. It follows, then, that a strong culture unified around a common purpose of high performance is a foundational part of a successful staffing firm. Like players on a professional sports team, a culture must be the glue that holds the team together while pushing them forward toward a shared goal. Cindy Pasky of Strategic Staffing Solutions summed it up by saying, "Culture is the fiber that weaves itself through every element of what you do as a corporation."

A unified culture is a force that influences all employees to join and make sacrifices toward a shared purpose. This is where the Disciplines of Commitment and Culture intersect. As stated in Chapter 3, an organization's Why is central to the Discipline of Commitment. From a cultural perspective, the Why unifies the culture by defining a shared purpose and acts as the glue that holds the culture together. Over time, the culture develops unwritten rules of what is and is not acceptable behavior, keeping the culture unified even as the company grows and becomes more complex. Leo Sheridan's quote provides insight into how a unified culture of performance is driven from the top and drives results through reinforcing the right attitude and behavior.

Chapter 5: The Discipline of Culture

Our culture has always remained constant with a focus on respect, excellence, accountability, and leadership. As a start-up, the culture is a by-product of the leader. A good culture is a culture of winning, of competition, of being a good teammate, and of having high respect for the players and the team itself. We were always aspiring to do great work and, at the same time, keeping each other accountable. At the end of the day, you've got to win.

—Leo Sheridan, Advanced Group

We believe the common saying that "culture eats strategy for breakfast" is particularly apt when it comes to staffing. A masterful strategy will fail if it is resisted by organizational culture. In addition, a mediocre or vague strategy can succeed if properly supported by a strong culture. Given two similar staffing firms, where one has a great strategy and one has a great culture, we would put our money on the firm with a culture unified around a common purpose.

Unfortunately, few organizations spend the time to build a winning culture focused on results. Instead, they end up with a culture by default, often focused on individual agendas. This creates a divided culture that distracts the team and weakens performance. Figure 5.1 contrasts a unified culture with a divided one to provide greater clarity into how they impact employee behavior and performance.

DIVIDED VS UNIFIED CULTURE

Figure 5.1

Divided Culture	Unified Culture
Lack of trust drives team members apart from one another and the management team.	Employees give each other and management the benefit of the doubt.
Conflict focuses on personal agendas.	Conflict focuses on enforcing standards and driving improvements.
Passive aggressive resistance to management direction.	Upfront communication and acceptance of the chosen direction.
Continuous finger pointing and gossiping.	Willingness to take accountability and hold others accountable.
Focus on individual needs.	Focus on results over individual agendas.

As seen in Figure 5.1, a unified culture aligned with a strong strategy leads to very powerful behavior, resulting in a Performance-Driven Culture that is not easily replicated by the competition. In this chapter, we will explore how a culture is initially formed and what is required to keep a culture strong as the organization grows.

Forming a Strong Foundation

That's my only real motivation, not to be hassled—that and the fear of losing my job. But you know, Bob, that will only make someone work just hard enough not to get fired.
—Mike Judge, Office Space[24]

While this scene from the comedy movie *Office Space* likely caused the audience to laugh, it undoubtedly carries an undercurrent of truth that should leave executives uncomfortable. If employees are not engaged, they will only give you the minimum amount of effort needed. While this attitude may be acceptable in monopolies or government agencies, it is dangerous in the world of staffing, where focus and motivation are crucial to competitiveness and long-term survival. To remain focused and motivated, employees need more than a manager telling them what to do. They need a culture they can identify with and believe in, a culture that unifies them with a common purpose.

Nearly every business leader has devoted a significant amount of time to budgeting and planning—not to mention days writing emails, creating spreadsheets, and building presentations. While these exercises must be done, they pale in comparison to the impact culture has on the growth of a staffing firm. In fact, we believe that the importance of a unified culture focused on performance is almost impossible to overstate. Yet how much time and energy goes into the critical work of establishing and forming the company culture? In most cases, the answer is "not enough," while in some cases, the leadership spends time on the culture but not in the right places. So what must leadership focus on to ensure that they are building a unified culture?

When interviewing top-performing staffing executives, we noticed that their cultures seem very different on the surface. However, a look at these cultures at a deeper level revealed three main similarities that together provide the foundation for a culture that both drives performance and successfully adapts as an organization grows. These three areas are alignment with competitive strategy, a shared belief system, and a result focused team.

ALIGNMENT WITH COMPETITIVE STRATEGY

As mentioned in Chapter 4, competitive strategy is defined by the customers a business chooses to serve and how that business differentiates itself from its competitors. The culture enables the execution of the strategy by promoting specific behaviors. To enable growth, these behaviors must align with the success factors of the competitive strategy. Employees in a unified culture inherently understand what behaviors drive competitiveness and what behaviors are unproductive or even destructive. If the culture is effective, they then police themselves and their co-workers accordingly. Fundamentally, culture enables execution of the strategy by defining what behaviors should be promoted and what behaviors should be discouraged.

For example, a consultative staffing firm relies on customer intimacy as a primary competitive advantage. However, customer intimacy represents a time investment from the client, which raises the client's expectation on the service level they are going to receive. Many consultative firms rely on a culture of collaboration to meet those expectations. Therefore, employees who are good collaborators are considered a better "cultural fit." In contrast, transactional firms often see too much collaboration as a waste of time, focusing more on quick and efficient interaction.

Culture plays a critical role in any competitive strategy. While some misalignment between the two is inevitable, there can be a tipping point where the misalignment eats away and undermines the cultural foundation. How do leaders help ensure that culture and competitive strategy stay in alignment?

The first step is for you to have a well-defined competitive strategy and a willingness to say no. Too many firms rely on opportunistic growth versus intentional growth that is guided by a competitive strategy. As discussed in Chapter 4, these companies can grow, but after a while, the success factors of these clients diverge from each other. This inconsistency leaves the staffing company struggling to scale operational capabilities and leaves employees confused about the company's direction. A firm with a strong competitive strategy knows when to say no to the wrong clients and has the discipline to pursue clients that align with its competitive strategy.

The next step is for you to establish and reinforce competitive practices through policies, processes, and tools. An effective operation with the right competitive practices creates momentum that shores up the culture and makes it more resilient.

- **Policies** should reward and recognize the right behavior.
- **Processes** should create repeatable workflows that add predictability and momentum to daily activities.
- **Tools** should enable the communication and enforcement of policies and the efficiencies of processes.

These are the details of the business that many executives do not enjoy. However, poorly constructed policies, broken or inconsistent processes, and outdated tools increase team frustration. As this frustration builds, it breaks the unity of the culture by undermining trust in leadership. The role of establishing and reinforcing competitive practices will be explored further in Chapter 7.

In addition, company structure also plays a crucial role in aligning culture with the strategy. The company structure largely determines how the chief executive communicates and interacts with their team. Effective communication allows leaders to convey their passion for the business while, at the same time, providing consistent messaging.

Some organizations can drive performance through aggressive top-down accountability. The effectiveness of that approach is limited to organizations filled with highly competitive employees who desire structure. Other organizations that prioritize innovation and problem solving have a looser structure that focuses on collaboration over compliance. Neither of these approaches is right or wrong. They are just different philosophies derived from the values and priorities of the chief executive and reflect how they want to lead as well as the needs of the competitive strategy.

A culture cannot drive growth if it is not aligned with the competitive strategy. Working with the right clients, establishing practices to reinforce the right behavior, and selecting the proper structure help ensure that a culture that focuses on the right behavior can be established. However, while alignment is critical to effective execution, it is shared beliefs that provide the glue that holds the culture together.

SHARED BELIEFS

At its core, we believe culture is a combination of a shared belief system and a common goal. Culture provides the unwritten rules of team behavior and plays a large role in defining how teams collaborate and focus on results.

Some examples of these unwritten rules include how employees handle conflict, what is expected of them, and how they hold each other accountable. Each one of these unwritten rules is not built on formal policies but on mutual expectations. This definition is persuasive because it highlights that even in the most unstructured companies, there are rules that govern behavior, even if they are unspoken. The question is whether those rules support or hinder company performance. The right shared beliefs ensure that the rules employees follow are consistent with the needs of the company.

The need for shared beliefs has been known for decades and is one of the drivers for companies to create the mission, vision, and values of an organization. An effective mission states what problems the company solves in the market or why a company exists. The vision provides the aspirational future state of what the company dreams of becoming, and values provide the behavioral context in which the team is to achieve that future. By creating the mission, vision, and values, leaders believe they have laid the foundation for a shared belief system the team can rally around. For many, those words are then put on placards but rarely spoken of again.

In these cases, leaders make the mistake of thinking the mission, vision, and values are an end in and of themselves. Instead, they are a means to an end. From a cultural perspective, they are meant to strengthen the personal connection an employee has with the company and to inspire them to be part of a team. But the mission, vision, and values must be personal to have their intended impact. It is the personal connection that energizes the culture by reinforcing that employees are not cogs in a bureaucratic wheel but instead are part of something exceptional.

The answer to achieving that level of adoption begins with the Power of Why, which we discussed in Chapter 3. Your organization's Why acts as the anchor point for the culture and provides critical insight for employees to answer the following questions:

- What do we care about?
- What makes us better than the competition?
- Why do I work here?

The answers to these three questions capture what the employees truly believe about the company where they work. Answers that are both positive and consistent represent strong shared beliefs that act as a unifying force for the culture. Achieving this unity is a creative process that varies from company to company. *A truly great culture does not come from placards on the walls but is felt as soon as you walk through the front door.*

For instance, at Strategic Staffing Solutions, visitors know right away that they have entered a different sort of company—one strongly influenced by founder Cindy Pasky driving a green culture. This culture values each employee and aligns their success with core values that have not changed in over a quarter century of serving customers. Moreover, the company's green logo color has become a rallying cry that permeates nearly everything about the company. As Cindy says, "All green, all the time." In addition, she consistently reinforces the message that they want to build a company that punches above their weight and refuses to be intimidated by other larger players.

Tom Gimbel of LaSalle Network provides another example: "When you walk into our office, you think that this place is electric. Our office has a really bright, upbeat feel to it and is decorated like a dot com. We have the bright colors; we have TVs on the walls and a wide-open lobby. Visually, you see bright lights and neon green. We also have a high interview volume with candidates walking around, so there is a buzz in the air. We really hire for culture."

Each executive we spoke with understands the importance of culture and invests time and energy to reinforce the answers to the three questions. Oftentimes, the answers to those questions are as simple as being a fun place to work, while others aspire to loftier goals. Regardless, these executives create an environment where there is an instinctive belief in the company and its direction. They want to succeed not only for themselves but to build an organization they are personally connected with and believe in. While the mission, vision, and values may provide important focus, they are simply insufficient to establish shared beliefs, as words by themselves are unable to connect on a personal level.

One of the most powerful results of shared beliefs is a team that can relate to one another and, therefore, trust one another. But why is trust important, and how does it drive a Performance-Driven Culture? Both those questions will be addressed in the next section.

THE RESULT FOCUSED TEAM

Trust lies at the heart of a functioning, cohesive team.
Without it, teamwork is all but impossible.
—Patrick Lencioni[25]

Patrick Lencioni is the founder of The Table Group, a management consulting firm that has worked with thousands of executives focusing on leadership and organizational health. One of his most influential books, *The Five Dysfunctions of a Team*,[26] identifies trust as the foundation for teamwork. He defines team trust as "the confidence among team members that their peers' intentions are good." Shared beliefs allow trust to take hold since intentions are not only understood but largely shared. The Lencioni model captures the domino effect trust can have on team behavior, including productive conflict, commitment, accountability, and the ability to focus on results.[27]

The opportunities for conflict in staffing occur every day, especially between sales and recruiting. Many people look at conflict as negative and, therefore, something that should be avoided. We believe that productive conflict is critical to success in staffing. Avoiding conflict leads to poor communication, lack of problem solving, and oftentimes passive aggressive behavior. The latter leads to gossip and other negative actions that gradually undermine the culture. Instead, productive conflict that focuses on solving problems and not personal agendas must be embraced. This type of conflict can only be achieved and managed with a team that trusts each other. It is the productive conflict that achieves true commitment from all parties involved.

According to Lencioni, commitment is the ability for an individual to commit to a direction even if they may disagree with it. This is a critical component of a high-functioning team since most business decisions are not a question of black and white, and ultimately require the leader to make a call on direction. Employees who have a high level of trust and can have productive conflict understand the nature of difficult decisions and are willing to embrace a direction they may have fought against. Commitment not only allows the organization to move forward on complex problems, but it also strengthens accountability at all levels of the organization.

What is the heart of a high-functioning team? When most people hear the term accountability, they typically think in terms of how leaders hold their employees accountable to their responsibilities. While this type of accountability is important, peer based accountability is the heart of a high-functioning team. These teams have an elevated level of trust, embrace productive conflict, and are committed to decisions even if they are not in their personal short-term interest. In these firms, the ground rules of behavior are not only clear but reinforced through employees' daily interactions with each other. This creates a culture of accountability that strips away personal interests, allowing teams to focus more on company results.

For Jay Cohen at Signature Consultants, the concept of accountability is basic to who they are as an organization.

Accountability is a very critical part of our culture. To us, it is doing what we need to do and, most importantly, doing what we agree that we should be doing. We all strive to do what we say we are going to do. Telling somebody we are going to do something and not doing it is lying, plain and simple. I think that's where accountability is. It's accountability for yourself and accountability for your partners that we all do what we say we are going to do.

—Jay Cohen, Signature Consultants

We have also seen accountability play out in high-performing staffing firms where metrics are made highly visible and everyone knows how they rank within the organization in terms of production and results. This is particularly true at The Delta Companies, ALKU, Medix, and other high-performing firms, where daily results are written on the walls of the office and are highly visible and easy for employees to know who is performing and working hard. The visibility of results reinforces the importance of individual productivity by publicly recognizing exceptional performance.

So how do trust, conflict, commitment, and accountability lead to results for high-performing staffing firms? At the most basic level, they allow personal agendas to be set aside for the greater good of the organization. Employees are not spending energy on posturing, because they trust one another. They engage in conflict with good intentions and focus on solutions to problems over winning arguments. They set aside egos and are willing to commit to decisions that are made, understanding there is often no one right answer. Finally, they are willing to hold each other to standards and motivate each other to hit a common goal. This is the heart of a high-functioning team.

We have four pillars of leadership at Delta: trust, coaching, accountability, and emotional intelligence. First is trust. You cannot do anything until you have established trust.

—*Jeff Bowling, The Delta Companies*

While achieving a trust-based culture is a powerful competitive edge, it is also important to remember how difficult it is to sustain. These cultures can overcome many obstacles, but one thing they cannot tolerate are employees who push personal agendas and break down the bonds of trust in the organization.

We heard from many of our top-performing staffing firms about the importance of weeding out employees who were undermining an effective culture. As Tom Gimbel of LaSalle Network put it, "It is not about hiring the right people; it is about firing the wrong people."

Many top producers are difficult to manage, but part of effective leadership is learning to use different management techniques that meet the needs of each employee. However, there are some employees who, regardless of production, undermine the culture. This is a common and complex problem many staffing leaders face. While some leaders are adept at minimizing their impact, there are others who choose to ignore the problem due to the gross margin they contribute. As we have seen multiple times, eventually these individuals will undermine the culture of the organization as well as the authority of the leadership team.

A unified culture must have a foundation that supports the company strategy, pulls people together, and focuses everyone on what is needed to drive results. However, growth challenges the resiliency of the culture in a variety of ways. Because each culture is different, they all have unique ways in meeting those challenges. But one thing they do have in common is a team of committed ambassadors who communicate the culture and protect and reinforce it against a variety of threats.

Breaking Through: Creating Cultural Ambassadors

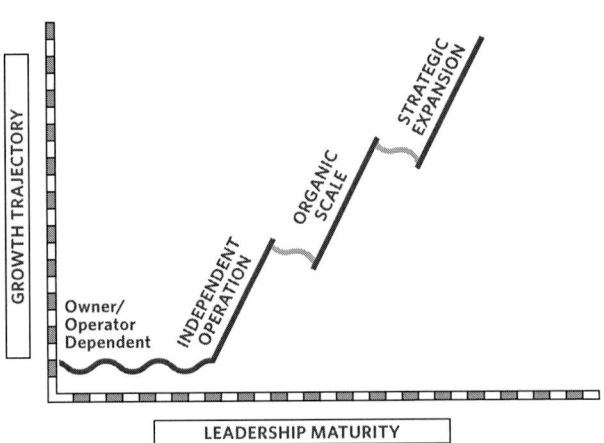

> *Keeping customers is about the experience, and the employees control the culture and temperature of the business. Never forget that.*
> —Steve Wynn[28]

Many top-performing founders view their company as an extension of their legacy, which in turn drives a passionate commitment to growth, as discussed in Chapter 3. At the Owner/Operator phase, the founder's commitment to growth lays the groundwork for a Performance-Driven Culture. During this phase, the founder provides a living example of the culture through their personality and the priorities they are continuously advocating. Employees model their behavior after this example and are often motivated by a combination of their personal relationship with the founder and the desire for recognition. However, it is during the Owner/Operator phase that much of the cultural foundation is laid. Because of this, you must ask yourself, "Is my culture scalable?" If the answer is no, the root cause is often due to the fact that the culture is driven by personality instead of a culture that is unified by shared beliefs.

For the firm that wishes to stay within the Owner/Operator phase, this does not pose much of a problem. However, growth provides challenges to a personality-driven culture as the founder begins to delegate leadership responsibilities and reduces their daily interaction with the team. With additional leadership managing much of the day-to-day, the culture is now impacted by the behaviors and priorities of multiple leaders with different personalities and management styles. How well the culture adjusts to this transition is directly related to the ability of new leaders to be ambassadors to advocate the culture.

As a company grows, the culture must evolve away from the personality of the founder and toward other leaders in the organization. The creation and empowerment of cultural ambassadors allows a culture to mature and scale. Each phase of growth provides unique challenges, but if those challenges are overcome, a more resilient culture will develop. A unified culture enables a firm to break through without sacrificing what makes it a unique and compelling place to work.

BUILDING AN INDEPENDENT OPERATION

The Independent Operation phase represents an important crossroads for a company culture. It is during this phase that line-level management truly becomes responsible for the day-to-day stewardship of the company. While much of this stewardship revolves around daily management duties, it is crucial not to underestimate the impact these managers have on the culture. These managers must become strong cultural ambassadors, but two things must happen first. The culture must become less reliant on the founder's direct daily influence, and managers must learn to become advocates for the shared beliefs of the organization. These shared beliefs can be formed very early in the company's existence, but for them to become established in the culture, they require buy-in from leaders at all levels of the organization.

Andrew Limouris describes how shared beliefs define both personal and professional relationships at Medix.

At the very beginning, there was purpose.

The things that we did for talent, the things that we did for our internal staff, and the things that we did for our clients were extraordinary. For example, a contractor would be driving to work and get a flat tire. It was natural for a couple of recruiters to go out to change the tire and buy the person a new tire. And that was in our DNA. During the early days in our company, my mom passed away. I went to the funeral in Greece. I got back, and I remember my team saying, 'Take all the time you need. We got your back.'

Still today we have a saying here that at 'Medix, we got your back.' We talk about showing up for people in good times and in bad. So that is a key trait, the core of our business. These values give us clarity of purpose. We know who fits in our company and who does not. This is not just limited to internal employees either; it translates to our partners as well.

Once I had a potential vendor say, 'Andrew, you know the purpose stuff you are talking about? You are just doing it to make money. You have to sell that stuff so your employees buy in.' Guess what. We did not give him the business. I never took his calls again. We know who we are; we know who we are going to lock arms with. It clears away all the people that are bringing black clouds over you.

Once you get to that point, it is just, 'Let's go, let's run.'

—Andrew Limouris, Medix

The most powerful and resilient belief systems are ones that are imprinted very early in the company's existence. For a leader such as Andrew, those beliefs are foundational to the culture. They provide critical context for almost all leadership decisions as well as employee behavior. They are also clear and personal, making them easy for other leaders to adopt as their own as well as promote within their teams.

These shared beliefs allow newly promoted leaders to unify the culture with or without Andrew's direct involvement. This unification energizes employees, motivating them to sacrifice and go the extra mile. There is no set of metrics or management system that can replace that mentality. As the Independent Operation continues to mature, it is not just formal leaders who drive the shared beliefs, but informal ones as well.

These informal leaders are part of daily conversations that reinforce the shared beliefs of the organization, both by example and by addressing competing narratives that nurture doubt and encourage cynicism. For most employees, standing up for the company is difficult since they risk the relationships they have with their co-workers. But for employees who embrace the shared beliefs, what the company stands for is more important than individual relationships. For that reason, they will help shore up the culture by pressuring those who seek to undermine it by either proactively reasserting positive messaging and/or successfully squashing destructive narratives before they build momentum.

The ambassadorship by formal and informal leaders allows the culture to further define itself and become a more and more powerful force within the organization. Tom Gimbel of LaSalle Network summed this transition up by saying, "The culture had surpassed what I as a founder could get it to be." A culture that achieves this level of maturity is both more resilient and more easily replicated, two factors that are crucial in achieving Organic Scale.

ACHIEVING ORGANIC SCALE

> *No person will make a great business who wants to*
> *do it all himself or get all the credit.*
> —Andrew Carnegie[29]

When it comes to building turn-key operations, most people immediately think about standard operating procedures, processes, and tools. While these are important in scaling an organization, their impact is limited if the culture cannot be effectively replicated. Each office or business unit must be led independently while, at the same time, being part of a unified culture.

The first step is the ability to trust the culture of remote branches to their local leaders. This is another level of delegation that is required in developing remote branches. Instead of delegating local leaders to reinforce cultural standards, they must delegate to a leader in a remote location that they will rarely visit. Many of our top-performing firms found that because of the critical need for local branch managers to have the culture as part of their DNA, they were most successful at relocating someone they already trusted as a cultural ambassador to build a new location. The trust they had, as well as their knowledge and acceptance of the company culture, more than made up for their lack of knowledge of the local community their branch office was seeking to develop.

Jeff Harris of ettain group provides his insight around both the challenges of delegating the culture and the eventual benefits.

I think leadership delegation is one of the biggest challenges founders face. As a founder, you are so emotionally tied to the business that allowing other people to set the tone of the organization directly challenges your mentality as an owner. However, in order to grow, you have to let go and trust your team.

As we began to add branches, we selected individuals who were part of our team to help us open those branches so we could grow as organically as possible. We really had to rely on our branch leaders to be cultural ambassadors for us.

There is no question that our success can be attributed to the leadership abilities of our management team. They are all so ingrained in the culture and committed to making the company successful that it just feeds down and drives the performance of their teams.

—*Jeff Harris, ettain group*

Jeff's approach to delegating the leadership of the culture reflects much of Patrick Lencioni's model, which is founded on the willingness and ability to trust. As Jeff tells it, "We hire people that we trust can do the job and give them the authority they need to do it." Dan Campbell of Hire Dynamics also referred to this approach to delegation by focusing on the communication of the "what" and trusting his team on executing the "how." This unstructured approach allows systems and processes to be relatively simple, empowering local leadership to build a culture that aligns with both their own style and the company as a whole. It also has an added benefit in elevating individual leaders and contributing to their personal growth and that of their team.

Often, leaders overmanage people because they do not trust that they can do the job. This mistrust manifests itself in overly burdensome management systems and metrics that attempt to shore up the perceived inadequacies of local leaders with systems and processes. But an overreliance on systems such as these sends an unintended message of mistrust to both the local leaders and the producers that their own judgment is inadequate. In addition, these types of solutions are an attempt to provide an operational solution to problems that are often fundamentally cultural by nature.

Leo Sheridan of Advanced Group recognizes the importance of truly understanding the challenges creating unified cultures within remote markets.

As we grew and started building businesses in different geographic markets, I needed to really get my brain around how to codify the culture so that we can make sure that we hire to it and that we can clearly articulate what the culture is and how it manifests itself in the behaviors that people demonstrate every single day. Once you start building beyond one location and one team you have to think through how to replicate what you've built into these new offices.

—*Leo Sheridan, Advanced Group*

Leo's quote covers a lot of ground. The first step is to truly understand your culture. The next step is to hire leaders who can represent the culture so it is properly articulated and drives the right behavior. Operational solutions are very limited in how they improve all those things and oftentimes make matters worse. For example, an overly rigorous top-down management approach can undermine the ability to build trust throughout all levels of the organization, thus removing productive conflict, undermining commitment, and ironically, stripping away accountability. Because of this, attempting to shore up leadership inadequacies through systems and processes can make any cultural problems worse.

In addition, executive reinforcement of the culture becomes even more important to ensure managers and their branches do not feel isolated. Some examples of executive reinforcement are site visits, company-wide contests, and kickoff meetings. For these events to have the intended effect, they must merge performance expectations with team building to make performance a fun and unifying goal instead of just a metric that needs to be hit to keep your job.

Ensuring cultural standards are reinforced as a company expands into Organic Scale requires a high level or awareness of what drives your culture and investing in leaders who can be independent ambassadors of that culture even if they are thousands of miles away. In addition, corporate leaders must look beyond operational solutions and provide cultural support to local branch managers to ensure the culture remains unified even as independent branches drive the company's organic expansion.

EXPANDING YOUR STRATEGY

Strategic Expansion requires the chief executive to consider that each strategy may necessitate a different culture. Due to that, cultural unification may need to be comprised. Any required cultural differences must be considered when determining how closely the existing and new operations should be integrated. As discussed in the previous chapter, when The Delta Companies expanded into Locum Tenens, the two niches did not require conflicting cultures, so the integration was relatively tight and cultural ambassadorship looked very similar from one group to another. Compare that to the companies that support both consultative and transactional staffing strategies. The success factors of each strategy are often so radically different that each require many of their own cultural norms. In these cases, cultural ambassadorship varies significantly from one strategy to another, so much so that the operations are often separated to allow each leader room to manage their culture differently.

The level of integration between cultures must also be considered when acquiring another firm. Some organizations purchase staffing firms and allow the existing management team to lead the organization as they see fit, providing financial goals are achieved. This approach is common among financial buyers, such as private equity firms who view their return on investment primarily through the growth of that individual firm. Therefore, there is no need to worry about the disruption of merging two cultures together.

Strategic buyers often purchase organizations with an eye specifically on integration. In this situation, successfully integrating the cultures represents one of the greatest challenges. Many purchases that initially look great are unable to effectively integrate because of the inability to bring the cultures together under a shared belief system. These are some of the cultural factors to take into consideration when expanding into new competitive strategies or acquisitions:

1. How dependent is Return on Investment (ROI) on the integration of the different firms?
2. How similar are the belief systems of different leaders?
3. How similar are the success factors?
4. Does the management approach have to vary?

One of the most successful staffing firm growth stories of all time is Allegis Group. The company has generated nearly all of its growth organically, going from start-up in 1983 to over $10 billion in 2016, making it the market share leader in the US staffing market.[30] In our opinion, Allegis is an excellent example of how a single strong culture can be scaled over time and the recognition by management that growing from within and focusing on organic growth as opposed to acquisitions is a more sustainable way to build an enduring staffing business. When Allegis did make acquisitions, a focus on cultural fit was a key part of their criteria.

Even though a new service offering or acquisition appears good on paper, it is important not to underestimate the cultural impact of these decisions. Strategic choices such as these can be highly disruptive to the culture of an organization and can damage overall company performance if not led appropriately. This includes deciding how closely the two groups need to work together and appreciating the level of cultural differences they will have to navigate. By ignoring the impact of these differences, leaders may encourage conflicts that undermine performance and can lead to employee turnover and business disruption. Regardless of how strong the new strategy is, always remember, "Culture eats strategy for breakfast."

Wrapping Up

While culture is important for companies of all industries, staffing companies depend on it as a key competitive differentiator. Even with all the changes in the staffing industry, it is still fundamentally a people driven business. How a staffing company performs is directly dependent on their individual producers. The more motivated and focused these employees are the more successful a staffing company will be. As a staffing firm grows, it is leadership's responsibility to ensure the culture grows with it. Strong cultural standards provide the leadership team the tools needed to reinforce the culture as the company maneuvers through the different phases of growth.

SUCCESS FACTORS FOR BREAKING THROUGH THE DISCIPLINE OF CULTURE

Figure 5.2

Transition	Creating Cultural Ambassadors
Building an Independent Operation	Establish strong belief systems founded on a well-defined vision and values that can be transferable to other leaders.
Achieving Organic Scale	Ensure local leaders have similar belief systems. Empower the leaders to become strong cultural advocates. Consider moving cultural ambassadors from existing markets to any new markets to ensure culture is consistent. Balance systems and the development of local leadership. Do not attempt to strengthen weak leaders through overly burdensome management systems. Be willing to replace leaders regardless of tenure when they undermine the culture.
Expanding Your Strategy	Structure the organization to support different cultural standards if needed. Integrate cultures by first ensuring leaders have similar priorities and belief systems. If cultural obstacles are inhibiting needed integration, either keep them separate or upgrade the leadership team.

BREAKING THROUGH

Chapter 6:
The Discipline of
Talent Development

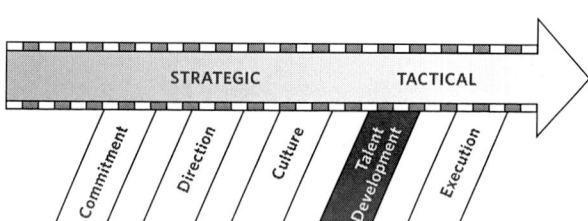

Those who build great companies understand that the ultimate throttle on growth for any great company is not markets, or technology, or competition, or products. It is one thing above all others: the ability to get and keep enough of the right people.
—Jim Collins[31]

In Chapter 4, we discussed the Discipline of Direction and how it provides the framework for both the targeted customers and the overall company structure. In Chapter 5, the Discipline of Culture focused on how a culture of shared beliefs ensures employees are committed to achieve results. These two disciplines along with the Discipline of Commitment act as the company's foundation and are fundamentally strategic in nature.

Once that foundation is in place, the tactical disciplines of Talent Development and Execution can now be addressed. This begins by ensuring the right people are in the right roles and that they are coached to execute those roles effectively. The identification and enablement of the right talent are the essence of the Discipline of Talent Development.

Bolstered by a strong, unified culture, Talent Development has proven to be an important differentiator for top-performing staffing firms for decades. In the previous chapter, we referenced Allegis Group's culture as a critical success factor to their growth. However, for a culture to scale, Allegis also had to master the ability to hire, coach, and promote employees. We believe Talent Development coupled with a strong culture allowed Allegis Group to grow organically from zero to over $10 billion in global revenue today. This makes them the largest staffing firm in the US, surpassing a number of competitors with much longer tenure in the industry.

That same focus on Talent Development enabled three former Allegis/Aerotek recruiters, who founded Apex Systems in 1995, to ultimately grow and sell the company to On Assignment for $600 million in 2012. In addition, a focus on growing and developing talent helped former Allegis recruiters take Insight Global from start-up in 2001 to over $1.6 billion in revenue by 2016.[32] Note the following statement proudly displayed on their website in 2017:

> *We are proud of the fact that since our inception in 2001, all promotions have come from within the organization. This model has played an integral role in developing a culture that fosters hard work, superior customer service, effective responsiveness and a deep care for our clients, our employees and the overall welfare of the company.*
> —*Insight Global, Core Principles*[33]

That is a remarkable statement for a $1.6 billion corporation. All promotions over the course of 15 years since Insight Global was founded have come from within the organization? How could that be true? Achieving something even close to that level of success in growing internal talent is remarkable. Being able to build the internal personnel to fuel growth from zero to $1.6 billion requires an intense focus on the Discipline of Talent Development.

The majority of top-performing staffing firms we interviewed also displayed a passionate focus on developing talent as a critical element of their growth. In the remainder of this chapter, we will explore what the Discipline of Talent Development looks like when it is consistently practiced as a top priority rather than being the afterthought seen in far too many organizations.

Building a Competitive Team

The fate of any staffing company is directly linked to its effectiveness at building competitive teams. This includes hiring, developing, and retaining the right internal talent. Building a competitive team is one of the most challenging responsibilities, and it is one that every leader within a staffing organization must commit themselves to. Mark Eldridge of ALKU summarizes how Talent Development has been a key focus for his organization.

From the very beginning, when we wrote our first five year plan, we realized that the biggest obstacle to our growth would be the ability to find, hire, and retain bright, motivated people. In fact, we have a saying that goes something like, 'When is the right time to hire a salesperson or a recruiter? Whenever you have found the right person.' From the very beginning, we focused on hiring revenue generating people whenever and wherever we could find them. We wanted to hire people who wanted a career, and the only way to retain people who want a career is to continue to grow as a company so that you can give them more opportunity.

—Mark Eldridge, ALKU

In this quote, Mark stresses that hiring is not something that should be dictated by plans or budgets but instead needs to be a constant priority. If you find the right person, simply hire them. Contrast this mentality with many staffing leaders who simply hire when someone leaves or when the hiring plan tells them to. Mark's approach is much more aggressive and proactive, highlighting the importance of talent to the long-term success of his business.

While it seems intuitive that the Discipline of Talent Development is something managers must embrace, it is often something they tend to ignore for more visible problems that occur on a day-to-day basis. To control the future growth of the company, staffing leaders must take an aggressive approach to strengthen internal talent by continuously asking themselves, "How do I make my team more competitive?" Many leaders do not know how to answer that question, and they are never able to proactively strengthen their most valuable asset: their team.

This section will focus on four components of Talent Development that leaders must execute to ensure they have the most productive team possible:

1. Assessment: Defining the capabilities your company needs and the roles necessary to fulfill them.
2. Hiring: Finding, screening, and onboarding talent to fill the necessary roles.
3. Coaching and Performance Management: Training new skills, improving performance, and motivating individuals and the entire team.
4. Promotion: Identifying and managing internal needs and candidates for advancement.

ASSESSMENT

Before knowing who to hire and how they need to be trained and developed, leaders need a clear understanding of the roles in the organization. Assessment is the starting point for every role in the organization by ensuring that they are defined by the proper expectations. David and Marty Luttrell from AtWork stressed the importance of defining the role of each position in their company.

One thing that has helped us is identifying our expectation of each position. Then you can hire the right person, hold them accountable, and make sure they know what is expected of them.
—David and Marty Luttrell, AtWork Personnel Services

These expectations include the key objectives of the role and the core competencies individuals must possess to meet those objectives. Objectives are the measurable success factors for any given role. They are used by management to measure employee productivity and often act as the benchmarks employees must reach to be successful. Objectives must be simple and easily managed by metrics. They can be developed for all roles, but they are most important for roles in management, sales, and recruiting. There are three types of metrics to consider: activity metrics (meetings, candidate screens); quality metrics (close rates, submittal-to-hire); and result metrics (head count, placements, gross margin). Depending on the role, it is not necessary to have all three, but it is important to identify at least one metric as the central performance quota for the role.

Quotas quantify the role's most important objective and should be used as the primary measure of success. Managers tend to conflate quotas with other performance metrics. However, while all quotas are metrics, not all metrics are quotas. For example, you may desire for a salesperson to make a certain number of calls a week. However, if that salesperson is hitting their placement and gross margin goal, are you going to put them on a performance plan if they are not hitting activity numbers? Experienced managers understand that while they may need to evaluate and manage to several metrics, there are typically only one or two that are actual quotas.

The following questions can be used to determine the quotas for any given role:
- Does the quota capture a critical deliverable of the role?
- If the employee consistently misses quota, does it warrant a performance plan or termination even if other metrics are in line?
- Is the quota simple to understand, accurately tracked, and consistently enforced? Are there ways to game the system that will conflict with the culture?

Once the objectives of the role are defined, the core competencies of the role have the proper context to be considered. Core competencies play a key role in the hiring process since they define the qualifications of any given position. There are three major types of competencies that determine the proper fit for a role: experience, aptitude, and suitability.

<u>Experience:</u> This captures the knowledge and proven skills a candidate brings to the table on day one. Experience is what we focus on when we are interviewing to explore a candidate's work history and discussing their accomplishments. In doing so, we are trying to validate that the experience is real and relevant to the role. While many firms value experience, some have set aside experience as a primary hiring criteria. This shift in priorities is partly due to larger staffing firms' inability to find enough experienced candidates to meet the headcount requirement. Additionally, many of our high-performing staffing firms prioritize aptitude and suitability over experience, as they believe it leads to a better cultural fit. They often build training programs to improve ramp-up time for inexperienced hires.

<u>Aptitude:</u> A person's ability to understand and apply new concepts and information can be thought of as aptitude. Aptitude is not only important in learning a new position; it is also a critical factor to a person's

adaptability. Much of aptitude is innate talent, making it difficult to screen for consistently. Assessments such as DiSC can provide some insight into a person's personality traits. Other assessments look for specific characteristics, such as motivation, drive, and resiliency. In general, if given the right amount of training and runway, employees with high aptitude will outperform lower-skill employees with more experience.

Suitability: Focuses on an individual's ability to embrace the company culture along with the competitive practices that drive day-to-day behavior. Suitability is not solely focused on personality fit, although it can be a consideration, especially for smaller firms. Suitability is something that is often overlooked. Regardless of a person's aptitude and experience, if they are not a cultural fit or choose not to adapt to the company's competitive practices, they can quickly become a liability. One way this liability can manifest itself is through someone who can bring in gross profit but is disruptive to both management authority and the company culture.

Going through the exercise of defining objectives and core competencies should be applied to all positions and for anyone who is applying to the role, even if they are internal promotions. Too often, producers are promoted not because they would thrive in the new role but because managers promote out of loyalty or fear of losing a top producer. A detailed assessment of the role can prevent managers from making a promotion for the wrong reason and reduce the chance of a mistake.

In addition, it is not just new roles that should go through this exercise. Assessing established roles can provide significant benefit since roles often need to evolve as the business evolves. For example, an account intially may require an aggressive account manager to develop relationships with hiring authorities. However, if a Managed Service Provider (MSP) is implementing strict rules of engagement, then that aggressiveness can become a liability.

Being politically savvy may now be a more important competency. Only with a proper assessment that defines what a role must provide, along with the needed competencies of that role, can a leader properly screen and hire the right personnel.

HIRING

To paraphrase Jim Collins in *Good to Great: Why Some Companies Make the Leap and Others Don't*, leaders need to get the right people on the bus and then make sure they are in the right seats. He also reimagines the old adage that people are a company's most important asset. As Collins puts it, "'People are your most important asset' turns out to be wrong. People are not your most important asset. The right people are."[34]

Jim Collins's sentiment rings even truer in the business of staffing, where people play a central role in all aspects of the business. It can be argued that the quality of their personnel is the most important thing that differentiates one staffing company from another. Having the right people on the bus sounds simple enough; however, as any leader can tell you, hiring the right people is probably the hardest job of any manager.

Ironically, while the staffing industry is based on helping people hire qualified individuals, many staffing leaders put less work into making their internal hires than the clients they support. It is the classic adage of the cobbler's children who have no shoes. When someone provides a service for a living, they often ignore the need of that service for themselves. We often see staffing leaders struggle to make hiring a priority. It is difficult to pin down where this tendency comes from, but it is real and is a common reason why firms underperform.

The example of ALKU shows a relentless focus on hiring great talent as perhaps its most important priority. Top staffing leaders approach hiring differently at a fundamental level. They do not view hiring as a dreaded task ripe for procrastination. Instead, they view it as a foundational asset that requires investment in both time and money. If the asset is weak, the company will fail. If the asset is strong, the company will grow. While most staffing leaders would agree with that concept, the question then becomes, how do executives with all their other responsibilities keep hiring a front and center priority?

The first success factor for hiring is focus. We live in a time where managers are bombarded with information. We have data to manage the day-to-day operations. We have data to review financial performance. We have data to diagnose operational issues. We have data to manage the performance of leaders and individual producers. While all this information provides value, it can easily become a distraction, pulling leaders away from important issues and into rabbit holes of relatively meaningless and minor problems.

Top-performing staffing leaders know that even though data is important, staffing is still a people business. People are the biggest expense, and people drive top-line growth. This leads to two questions staffing leaders and their managers must ask themselves:

- Do we have the right people in the right roles?
- Are we filling the right roles to drive future growth?

These two questions force managers to be held accountable for the most important aspect of their job, strengthening their team through proactive sourcing.

Most managers tend to ignore sourcing until they must respond to a major event, such as landing a new account, launching a new line of business, or dealing with staff turnover. Proactive sourcing takes a preemptive and opportunistic approach to hiring talent. Instead of starting the hiring process when an open position becomes available, leaders who source proactively are continuously looking for new talent. Andrew Limouris of Medix said, "Never stop trying to find good talent. When you find someone, even if there is no opening in your company, hire the person." Proactive sourcing not only allows managers to reduce the impact of unexpected turnover but also increases the likelihood of finding top talent merely by exposing the manager to more candidates.

As leaders, our job is to build the most competitive team possible, not to settle. The ability to hire talent is not only necessary to grow the organization, but it also empowers leaders to replace people who are either unproductive or damaging to the culture. Often, leaders hold on to people too long, not out of altruism but because of a lack of preparedness. They have not been building a pipeline of new talent and, therefore, do not have any better options. This reluctance is not a reflection of values but instead a refusal to proactively build the best team they can assemble.

Of course, maximizing the return on proactive sourcing needs to be coupled with a strong interview process. There is no one hiring process that all top staffing companies follow, but there are certain practices that they all have in common.

The first is clearly understanding all the competencies that are needed to work in your organization. Most leaders understand how to screen for skills and experience but often ignore aptitude and suitability. It is critical that you understand and interview for all these traits, which can include understanding a candidate's value and personality characteristics. Experienced managers who consistently interview become skilled at both communicating why these traits are important and identifying them during the interview process.

Dan Campbell of Hire Dynamics summarized the importance of hiring for important criteria when he said, "If you don't get the hiring right, nothing else matters. You can have the best core values, the best mission and vision statements, but if you aren't hiring to them, then you will never get any traction on developing the culture you want to achieve."

The second practice is to have a hiring process that can be thorough but not overly complex and burdensome. In addition, the process must match the experience level of the candidates being considered. For example, many firms source their talent directly out of college. These companies have two challenges to address in this process: first is to screen for aptitude and suitability; second, they must educate the applicant on the nature of the industry to avoid high turnover rates.

To accomplish both these objectives, a number of high-performing firms have candidates shadow their employees for a few hours or an entire day. By shadowing, these candidates see firsthand the work required to succeed in the staffing industry. The employees also get to interact with them on the floor and observe their aptitude and suitability for the job. While this practice helps both the company and the candidate screen each other, it is obviously not appropriate for experienced candidates who already understand the industry.

An extension of shadowing is creating internship programs. Mark Eldridge at ALKU and Jeff Bowling at The Delta Companies both have employed college interns as a way to build a pipeline of talent. This is also a low-risk approach to evaluate suitability for the company before offering candidates a full-time position.

It would be difficult to find a more common and more expensive mistake than mis-hires. It is not uncommon for a staffing company to have less than 50% of their new hires still with the company six months later.

This low success rate reflects a poorly focused hiring process, though poor retention may also reflect additional problems with how teams are motivated and developed.

COACHING AND PERFORMANCE MANAGEMENT

> *Each person holds so much power within themselves that needs to be let out. Sometimes they just need a little nudge, a little direction, a little support, a little coaching, and the greatest things can happen.*
> —Pete Carroll, Head Coach, Seattle Seahawks[35]

Outside of hiring the right people, it would be difficult to identify a more important responsibility for managers than coaching their teams. Successful coaches are a source of knowledge and inspiration. They motivate their teams and provide them the guidance neccesary to become more competitive. In staffing, where individual performance drives growth, teams need to be knowledgeable and highly motivated. For that reason, great staffing leaders are typically also great coaches.

One of the problems organizations have is understanding what an effective coaching program looks like. Coaching is a combination of training and motivation. Training focuses the development of employees' skills as well as their overall professional maturity. In addition, effective coaching motivates individuals to improve. This motivation is driven both culturally and through one-on-one engagement. We will discuss the importance of training programs and motivation later in the chapter.

As mentioned in the previous chapter, company culture plays a central role in reinforcing desired behavior. A culture that openly advocates for professional development is one that will more likely have employees open to learning and self-improvement. Jeff Bowling highlights how training has been a central part of the culture at Delta.

I'm an avid learner. I love to read and to get better. I'm not going to outsmart a lot of people in the room, but I can out-prepare them. And that's been my personal strategy most of my life, just out-preparing other people. That's why I really believe in training. Last time I checked, we did three times the amount of training that an average company in our general inside sales staffing space would do.

It's hard for me to believe, but not a lot of people really value training. For some, it's just a necessary evil or an interruption to their day, and it's not embedded into the organization. We provide centralized training on topics like salesmanship, industry knowledge, time management, writing emails, and other very practical things. We even do things like how to buy a house for first-time homebuyers and how to be a better parent, because it's just built into the culture.

We have sales clinics every day. You may not have to go every day, depending on your level and your recent performance, but we have these sales clinics, and they are practical, real world ways to get better at your job.

—*Jeff Bowling, The Delta Companies*

Jeff's investment in training sends the message that learning is essential to success, and not just in business but in our personal lives as well. This message makes training not just something a person has to do but a value that requires commitment from both the company and the employee. This is a cultural message that employees can embrace, influencing not only their willingness to learn and adapt but to teach others when the opportunity arises.

When both management and employees value training at this level, it maximizes the return on both formal and situational training. Formal training provides foundational knowledge through planned events and topics, typically in a group environment. The need for formalized training increases as a company grows, as discussed by Leo Sheridan of Advanced Group.

When you are $150 million and you have 360 employees and want to grow to 500, it's time to find a person to lead your people strategies. With the acceleration of our hiring, we needed to build a world-class training program in order to develop producers to profitability as quickly as possible.

We've developed classroom and e-learning training systems and processes that now give us a high probability that people will be producing successfully within six months. This is a tough decision to make because the investment is huge. Either stay the course and have your managers coach to success informally or put a structured program in place. The issue as you grow is that, one day, you wake up and realize that informal and ad hoc training on its own is not going to cut it.

—*Leo Sheridan, Advanced Group*

When it comes to real world application, formalized training must be supplemented by situational training. Situational training bridges theory and practice by taking events as they occur and using them as learning opportunities. As Leo indicates, both types of training play an important role in developing talent.

The other important aspect of coaching is motivation. Staffing is a tough business, and employees are very prone to burnout. Great coaches understand how to motivate people individually and as a team. Providing this energy is a crucial test in a manager's leadership skills. For many of our top-performing firms, motivation was a significant focus of senior management attention. Many of the top-performing firms are also highly rated on SIA's ranking of the Best Staffing Firms to Work For, which measures employee engagement with their work.

Of course, the question could be asked, "Do these companies have high levels of employee engagement because they are growing, or are they growing because of the level of engagement?" There is no doubt that when times are good, most teams are self-motivating. Aside from the financial benefits, success builds confidence, and confidence feeds morale. But as anyone who has been in this business more than a few years knows, staffing is highly cyclical and the good times will not last forever, regardless of the company. Eventually, either a client is going to disappear or the market will soften, bringing a new set of challenges to the production team. It is at this point that they are looking for credible leaders to keep them focused and motivated, and they will most likely mirror the behavior they witness from their leaders. If they perceive their leaders as unsure, they will lose confidence and begin to question the direction of the company. If they see a credible confidence, they will mirror that confidence as well.

All producers want to have confidence that their leadership team is in control of the fate of the company and will address problems in a timely and decisive way. But leadership credibility is not something that can be switched on by a single speech. It is something that is developed and cemented over time, and then when needed, can instill confidence in the team. Motivation and credibility are tightly linked. Ineffective leaders may be personally liked but lack the credibility to inspire confidence during difficult times—the times when their leadership is needed most.

PROMOTION

If there is any one indicator of how well an organization is hiring and coaching their team, it would be successful promotions of internal staff. However, effective hiring and coaching does not ensure that the right people will be promoted. It is natural for leaders to promote employees based on tenure or performance, especially when these very people expect to be promoted. Promotion to a leadership role is a risk, and the wrong decision can result in losing the promoted employee while causing turnover and disruption in the group they are managing. To manage that risk, leaders must develop a sense of what makes a good leader within their organization. While every job requires different skills, there are some common characteristic to look for in leaders.

Complementary Leadership Style: It is human nature to want to hire people like you. While all sorts of people can become successful, among our top-performing firms, we saw more examples of leaders who found a successful partner or leadership team with complementary skills than those who hired teams that were more or less clones of their own skills and style. Yes, whoever you hire absolutely should share your values and vision, but successful leaders also should seek to develop a team where people of varying strengths and interests can thrive.

Complementary relationships create an environment where weaknesses are shored up and strengths can be fully developed. A common example of this is a sales driven executive who may consider bringing in a leader who understands and is passionate about operations and delivery. This allows the executive to still drive the sales strategy and influence the culture while having someone who can identify any operational bottlenecks that could inhibit growth. Complementary leadership styles provide a more well-rounded understanding of not just internal operations but the client base as well.

A great example of leaders complementing each other was seen in the interview with David and Marty Luttrell from AtWork. These partners share a similar vision but have complementary skills that have helped their company to grow.

Marty will tell you that the best thing he ever did was come to work for me, and the best thing I ever did was hire him. Marty's strategic approach to the business complements my operational focus. It has been a good fit for both of us since our strengths make up for each other's weaknesses.

—David Luttrell, AtWork Personnel Services

While David is more operational and makes sure everything is in order, I am a big picture person. When I came on, I started looking at the financials from a strategic standpoint, identifying savings in the overall cost structure, which has given us more flexibility for growth.

—Marty Luttrell, AtWork Personnel Services

Another example of complementary leadership occurred during Organic Expansion when Marty and David Luttrell successfully identified a VP of Sales. They promoted a loyal employee, who they said was "not intimidated by anyone and was a very good addition to our team. She has credibility within the culture and is well respected." Her strong personality was needed to hold the sales team accountable and helped strengthen the entire leadership team.

<u>Temperament of a Leader</u>: One of the most common mistakes a chief executive can make is assuming that a top producer has the temperament to become an effective leader. But leadership requires different skills than those of an individual contributor. For leaders to be effective, they must be patient. They must defer recognition. They must advocate positions they may not personally agree with. They must be careful how they show emotions. They must set priorities for the company. In addition, they no longer have direct control over their compensation. Some of these characteristics are in direct contrast to what drives many top producers, thus setting some up for failure before they even spend their first day on the job.

It is understandable to want to promote top producers. They have instant credibility as someone who can get the job done. It is assumed that since they are successful, they should be able to spread that success to others. While many top producers can make a successful transition to leadership roles, success is by no means guaranteed. It is important to evaluate their leadership skills as needed in the new role.

In some cases, we have seen organizations promote top producers who are suffering from burnout in order to retain them. Not surprisingly, in most cases, burnout is a terrible reason to promote someone—not the least of which is that it blinds people from the reality of the burdens of management that require a specific type of temperament. While top producers can become effective leaders, many end up failing. In these cases, the company is hit twice. They lose their top producer, and they have set their teams back months or, in some cases, years. The smarter move is to coach for burnout, identify options for key producers, and then take more time to identify potential leaders and develop them for when your organization needs them.

The least profound cliché in our industry is that great salespeople don't always make great sales leaders. I think it's a bit more complex than that. You must know why people were successful in sales to know whether they can be a good leader or not. So one of the other things you have to learn is how to identify talent. You have to identify sales talent who will be able to make the transition to sales leadership. There is a difference between someone who was successful because they had a cushy account versus someone who really had to work at it. You can't scale good accounts, and you can't scale somebody who just has an innate ability to sell. They have to know why they were able to go produce gross margin. That you can scale.

—Jeff Bowling, The Delta Companies

Instead of looking at production as the primary criteria for leadership, it is critical to identify an individual's natural inclination toward the role by asking the following questions:

- Can they influence and motivate their peers?
- Are they energized by team success as well as their own?
- Are they effective communicators?
- Will they accept accountability for mistakes, or do they deflect blame?
- Do they recognize the success of others?
- Do they have a passion for their own development?

Adaptable and Coachable: New managers seldom automatically and naturally know what they are doing, even if they have been given a three page job description with succinct bullet points on day-to-day activities. New managers learn by doing their job and getting situational training from a mentor. For training to be effective, new managers cannot be defensive; they have to be willing to take feedback in an objective way. Of course, the chief executive plays an important role in setting the proper tone, holding the new manager accountable while providing the right amount of freedom to develop his or her own leadership style.

It is one thing to promote a leader with all these qualities, but what about the high-value employees who are not management material? A leader must be honest with their employees about their strengths and weaknesses, and then if possible, identify a role that better suits the talents of the employee. As a leader of a fast-growing organization, Jay Cohen of Signature Consultants accomplished just that.

Some of our greatest people started as salespeople and then became managers, but they were not effective in the management roles. I focus on the personal level and tell them it does not mean that they are not great. It is just that they are not in a role where they can reinvent themselves and be happy and successful. We have helped people reinvent themselves. For example, one of our valued team members had a strong background as a recruiter and a salesperson. At a point in time, we asked him to be a manager, not only was he not happy, but also it was clearly not the right fit. In a new role, he has now totally transformed our data analytics, manages a staff of five, and is happy.

—Jay Cohen, Signature Consultants

The ability to objectively evaluate your internal talent and act upon those assessments is one of the hardest skills to master for a staffing leader, but it is also the skill that provides the greatest return.

Jay understands the types of roles his company needs in order to be successful. He also pays close attention to the skills and personality characteristics of the people he promotes. Too often, leaders focus solely on the need to fill the position, but they do not effectively evaluate the people they are putting into those roles. This assessment is not just about skills and knowledge but is also around the needs of the employee, many of which are personal in nature.

The Discipline of Talent Development begins with clearly defined roles, which in turn, provide clarity for the capabilities needed. Only then can the right candidates be hired. Of course, even the best employees need coaching, since it both strengthens their fundamentals and broadens their skill set. Finally, the ability to promote internal talent enables faster delegation of management responsibilities while improving internal retention.

Each leader has different strengths and weaknesses when it comes to assessment, hiring, coaching, and promotion. The chief executive must understand the strengths and weaknesses of their leaders and coach them to be effective in all four areas. The ability to break through is dependent on giving leaders greater responsibilities and providing them the training necessary to execute those responsibilities effectively. As we see in the next section, this is true in all phases of growth.

Chapter 6: The Discipline of Talent Development

Breaking Through: Elevation and Delegation

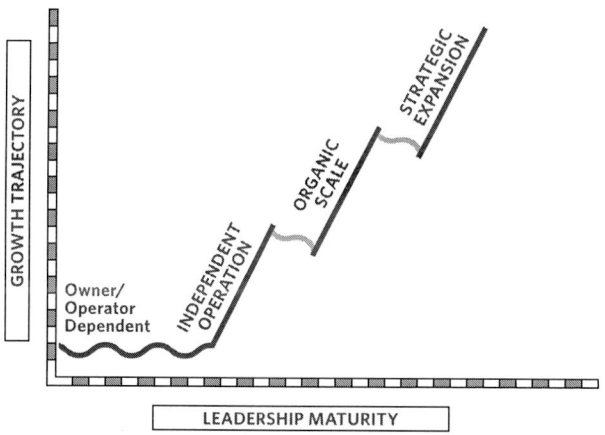

At the Owner/Operator phase, the founder wears a lot of different hats. They are the top producer, the trainer, the manager, and the chief executive. Over time, the founder begins to delegate production, typically by handing over accounts to more junior-level salespeople. As the company continues to grow, the founder gets pulled into more and more client and operational problems. These problems begin to dominate the day-to-day job of the founder, and other parts of the business begin to suffer, often starting with Talent Development.

Unfortunately, lack of focus on Talent Development can create a cycle of tactical firefighting as the Owner/Operator rushes hiring and cuts corners on coaching. Now the founder has created another problem: an unproductive team. Personnel issues force the founder to become even more involved in the day-to-day, making the operation even more dependent on them.

To break or avoid this cycle, the Discipline of Talent Development must be a priority even at the company's earliest phase. No longer can the Owner/Operator fix every problem. Instead, they must focus on elevating their team and delegating certain day-to-day responsibilities. Fundamentally, a leader who is consumed by the present cannot effectively build for the future. Talent Development addresses that problem by allowing leaders to build an organization where tactical problems are largely delegated, enabling the company to become more and more independent.

BUILDING AN INDEPENDENT OPERATION

As a company moves from the Owner/Operator to the Independent Operation phase, the first step in Talent Development is the identification, promotion, and development of the first line-level managers. This role represents the first time there is a manager between the executive and the production team. Whether an executive hires someone from the outside or promotes internally, the establishment of a day-to-day operational leader poses change management challenges that can impact every aspect of the organization. No longer does the production team have direct access to the executive; instead, they now have an intermediary. This fundamentally changes the relationship the employee has with both the executive and the company.

This delegation of certain elements of Talent Development to the new managers represents an important crossroads for the chief executive. The main obstacle at this phase has more to do with the executive learning to delegate than the complexity of the problems. New leaders will have a different style, will identify different problems, and will craft different solutions that the chief executive may or may not agree with. Leaders must balance delegation with the desire to implement their own solutions. By doing so, they provide an environment for the new leaders to grow and become more independent while minimizing risk in the organization. It is important to keep in mind, the level and timeline of responsibilities that are delegated can vary based on their strategic nature and complexity.

Coaching is typically the first responsibility to be delegated to the new line-level manager. In fact, there are many cases where a firm creates a team lead role whose only true management responsibility is the training of more junior-level personnel. Depending on the leadership abilities of the new manager, motivation can be a major hurdle. This is especially true for someone who has been promoted and is now leading former peers. Because of this, motivation is one area where the executive should still be involved through team communication and one-on-one interaction. Eventually, as the new manager gains experience and credibility, they will be able to play a more direct role in motivating their team.

New managers must be able to assess their team members. Having an established performance review process is ideal, but if there is not a process, the chief executive should work with the new manager to establish one. The performance review process provides a platform for new managers to coach and exert authority for underperforming employees who may need to be terminated.

Many line-level managers struggle with termination and tend to hold on to unproductive employees for too long. In addition, there may be employees the chief executive wants to postpone firing, thus hamstringing new managers. For these reasons, constant communication is crucial between new managers and the chief executive regarding the internal talent pool. These conversations will naturally evolve into the next responsibility: hiring.

Selecting talent is a skill that requires time and practice to become proficient. New managers should be involved with any hire for their team. Their involvement strengthens accountability for the success or failure of that new person. Regardless of available head count, the new manager should be consistently interviewing, not only to have a pipeline of available talent but to understand the state of the candidate market.

The selection of next level managers, along with the appropriate amount of involvement from the executive, is critical in ensuring an effective transition to an Independent Operation. As new managers become more skilled in the assessment, hiring, coaching, and promotion of talent, those practices can then be replicated and become part of the foundation for the company to achieve Organic Scale.

ACHIEVING ORGANIC SCALE

In achieving Organic Scale, the most important step is identifying the right leaders to build new operations. Many of our top-performing staffing firms found that the best way to ensure that culture is transferred to new operations was by internal promotions or transfers of successful leaders from existing operations. The promoted talent has certain advantages because they understand the culture and processes, and have existing relationships with other members of the leadership team. If no one is ready or willing to be promoted, hiring from the outside can be effective but does require more oversight from the executive to ensure the new leader understands how the company works and is assimilating effectively.

When trying to achieve Organic Scale, the Discipline of Talent Development requires more structure and formality to ensure consistency and scalability. Many companies go overboard with structure and centralization, which takes authority and accountability away from remote managers. Achieving that right balance is critical in ensuring a strong and scalable discipline.

In the Organic Scale phase, the manager's ability to independently assess the state of their internal talent must mature relatively quickly. This is not just about evaluating current employees. At the Organic Scale phase, it also includes forecasting what roles the operation needs to grow and then achieving that growth.

When levels of management are added, new measures and systems must be established to ensure senior leadership has the necessary visibility to oversee the productivity of their teams in multiple locations. In addition, performance reviews should have a level of consistency both in frequency and in the metrics that are reviewed. Variances in metrics may be required based on the size of the different operations, the nature of the market, and the experience level of the team. This shared management approach, along with a level of flexibility, allows managers to collaborate more effectively while not being overly restricted by a one-size-fits-all management system. This balance between structure and flexibility is a recurring challenge that will also be addressed in the next chapter.

Chief executives at this phase may consider adding another layer of management to support more operations. At this point, the organization must decide whether it will be a matrixed organization or a traditional hierarchical one. The most common matrixed organization incorporates either a Vice President of Sales or Vice President of Recruiting role to whom production personnel in remote branches report to as well as their day-to-day manager. This structure allows functional knowledge and coaching to be shared throughout the organization as well as countering possible weakness of local leaders. A hierarchical structure is where the local managers report to a regional manager who provides them the coaching and guidance they need to manage and develop their team.

Regardless of the type of organizational structure, we believe that leaders should keep the organization as flat as possible.

Another common challenge in the Organic Scale phase is the impact turnover has in building the production team. When an organization is a single physical operation and the chief executive is involved with the team, turnover can stay relatively low. However, with the addition of remote offices, the turnover rate typically increases, especially when bringing in a large volume of new talent. The combination of high turnover and a larger team size makes it a challenge just to keep the team at status quo, much less grow.

To address increased turnover, many organizations begin to involve Human Resources in the sourcing and, in some cases, the onboarding of new talent. This allows the organization to create more strategic sourcing strategies as well as free up the line-level managers to focus their time on current production.

We have a huge emphasis on who we are hiring to make sure they are the best possible people. We can have the best strategy in the world but without the right people we know we are not going to grow at a rate that is optimal. It is critical to our growth and our success.

—*Andrew Limouris, Medix*

In this example, Andrew emphasizes the investment and focus necessary in hiring in the Organic Scale phase. This emphasis includes the establishment of a structured hiring methodology and the provision of corporate support to assist in building the internal pipeline of candidates. Having a hiring methodology provides a consistent process to evaluate candidates, while the pipelining relieves the line-level manager of that time-consuming responsibility.

Just as employee evaluation is strengthened through standardization during the Organic Scale phase, so are onboarding and coaching. For organizations that hire junior-level personnel, getting them up and running quickly is a labor intensive effort. Combine that workload with a relatively high turnover rate, and it is easy to understand why a coaching program focusing on the first 90 days can provide significant value to the organization. Ongoing training can be developed internally and/or can be provided by an outside vendor. Regardless of the approach, a robust, more formalized training program can be very effective in improving ramp-up time as well as reinforcing company culture, values, and best practices.

Achieving Organic Scale also creates challenges in motivation. While local managers play the most important role in motivating employees, they cannot fight the tendency for a branch office to feel remote and disconnected from their peers. To increase buy-in and loyalty to the company, it is important to have corporate recognition to bring the company together. Most of the high-performing firms we studied had a combination of monthly, quarterly, and annual awards where exceptional producers are recognized for their performance.

Monthly or quarterly company updates can also provide the chief executive an opportunity to educate the team about the state of the company while, at the same time, helping employees feel a part of the larger organization. These meetings can be conducted at the corporate location or at alternate branch locations, thus giving the executive the opportunity to meet with the remote teams in person. The latter approach is a very effective way to address the potential alienation remote offices can perceive while, at the same time, giving top leadership a cursory evaluation of the branch.

Training programs also tend to go through the process of standardization, where corporate shared services take a greater role in how new employees are onboarded and how ongoing training programs are conducted. We saw earlier in the chapter, with Jeff Bowling of The Delta Companies, where weekly trainings driven by corporate alleviate much of the training load from the local manager.

When moving from an Independent Operation to Organic Scale, standardization provides the structure required for line-level leaders to develop their teams. In addition, these standards provide the framework for managers to collaborate with one another to assess how effectively they are developing their teams. Without standardization, managers are left to their own devices, which slows their development as managers and increases the likelihood of making mistakes that will undercut performance.

EXPANDING YOUR STRATEGY

As discussed in Chapter 3, breaking through the barriers to growth begins with commitment. This commitment begins with the executive team and their willingness to evaluate and address their weaknesses. Strategic Expansion often tests the adaptability and resolve of the executive team due to the different challenges it often brings to the table. This need for executive team development is especially true when expanding into new service offerings or competitive strategies. Executives are often presented with opportunities that are outside their current area of expertise. Education, executive coaching, attending conferences, or even just reading and studying business books are all ways that executives can develop greater strategic vision. Andrew Limouris of Medix focuses his development in many ways.

Everyone should have a coach or a mentor. I've had two during my time at Medix. We got a coach, and we started to follow their methodology. I think every team or any company should have a certain methodology in which they manage their business. One key to our success is that we never stop searching for that next coach or mentor. Once you stop learning, you stop innovating and you stop growing. You just kind of stop.

I try to read two books a quarter and find other ways to learn each quarter. It opens your eyes up to what's going on in the world. If you are not doing something every week to learn, you'll fail.

—*Andrew Limouris, Medix*

If the decision is made to pursue new strategies for expansion, then the next question is, "Do we have the talent to lead the new strategy?"

The answer is oftentimes no, requiring the executive to look outside their organization for a senior leader who can independently lead the execution of the strategy.

Hiring a truly independent leader to execute a new strategy often drives different approaches to all elements of Talent Development. The magnitude of that difference is based on both the leadership style of the new executive and the unique talent requirements of the strategy itself. While there are too many variations of how these differences may manifest themselves, some common differences are outlined below.

Organizations that have effectively mastered Organic Scale typically have a well-defined hiring philosophy and process. Strategic Expansion often challenges both existing assumptions on hiring profiles and the procedures in which they are brought on board. Depending on the scope of hiring that is dedicated to the new strategy, it may be necessary to significantly change both the hiring profiles and the hiring process. And while adjustments may be necessary, it is critical for the chief executive not to underestimate the impact they can have on the culture of the entire organization. If the executive is not careful, a competitive rivalry may form between the two teams, causing undue distraction that undermines performance.

In our interviews, Tom Gimbel of LaSalle Network discussed how hiring strategic talent can allow an executive to successfully take on other competitive strategies.

> *After having one of our internal employees start it, we hired someone to come in and focus on sales growth for our healthcare revenue cycle practice, which has been a huge success story for us. It has not only driven success in that sector but made us more adaptable and able to evolve to the changing marketplace.*

Also, hiring someone to manage our service business has changed how many of our biggest customers look at us. They are now committing teams of talent to us instead of just filling one job at a time.

—Tom Gimbel, LaSalle Network

Many executives struggle with delegation in general, much less delegating a growth strategy to another executive. When confronted with difficulties in a business that the chief executive is not familiar with, the tendency is to become overinvolved in challenging the strategy. In Gimbel's case, he made two significant hires and then gave them the runway patience required for them to succeed. He hired a leader for the healthcare practice, and he brought in a corporate resource to manage the services business. This corporate talent allowed LaSalle Network to modify its value proposition and provide bundled staffing solutions in addition to traditional staffing. This represented a shift in the niche LaSalle Network was able to support without radically having to adjust their operations. As with other hires, the key to success was the quality of the leaders he hired; everything else pales in comparison.

One of the most common threats to Strategic Expansion begins with ineffective evaluation of the roles needed for effective execution. Too often, the chief executive underestimates the scope of the differences between two strategies and decides to conflate the two strategies under a single team. A common example of this is adding professional services to the portfolio and attempting to use the same sales team to sell both projects and staffing. While some companies have seen some success with this model, many have seen their sales team become less and less productive. This negative impact on productivity is largely driven by the inability to communicate multiple messages and value propositions to the clients as well as managing two distinct sales processes. In addition, the skills required to sell staffing versus other services are different and often do not translate well to the new strategy.

These impacts can often be felt by the recruiting team as well if they are asked to support radically different delivery models. While recruiters can typically support a fairly wide range of positions, some strategies, such as project services, often require their own workflow as well as subject matter expertise that can interrupt the flow of the desk and negatively impact productivity.

A major advantage of the firm that has achieved Organic Scale is the opportunity to invest and create powerful turn-key training programs. Many of these programs were developed through trial and error over a period of years. It is easy for a leadership team to underestimate the amount of work involved in developing an effective program and, thereby, underestimate the amount of work required in developing training to support a new strategy for Strategic Expansion. This knowledge obstacle is made even larger by the fact that the institutional knowledge around the offering is often limited or nonexistent. For that reason, many firms focus their initial hiring on experienced personnel—the exception being when the new strategy requires significant head count. In that case, the development of a new training program becomes a critical strategic investment.

In addition to training their team, many of the top executives we spoke to were committed to their own development through networking and constantly learning as well as attending executive conferences and reading research, leadership, and general business material. While we see this commitment to their own development through all phases, it is especially critical in the Strategic Expansion phase, when making the choice to expand growth strategies because of the massive financial investment and operational ramifications of these decisions.

Many successful leaders also brought in outside advisory boards or peer groups to help with their development, which can also be particularly helpful during the Strategic Expansion phase. Executive advisory groups take different forms but provide essentially the same function. They all provide key external insight to identify strategic blind spots the executive may have as well as holding them accountable for making difficult but strategically crucial decisions. Jeff Harris of ettain group describes how his advisory board and board of directors influenced his strategic decisions as well as holding him accountable to those decisions.

When I brought in the advisory board, I was working through the idea that this is my baby, I do not want to screw it up, and I need some smarter people than me around me if I'm going to learn. Our advisory board has been very good about validating strategy and continuing to hold me accountable for making difficult strategic decisions. I needed someone to hold me accountable. When we get together every quarter, they want to see that I have done what I planned. If I did not do it, they want to know why. So the accountability for the strategy has been the biggest benefit of an advisory board. They prepared me for a private equity transaction and a new board of directors, which is an even greater level of accountability, and it has forced me to become a better executive, and ambassador for shareholder value.

—Jeff Harris, ettain group

While the training of the chief executive and employees needs to become more sophisticated, there are also issues with motivation that need to be addressed. As mentioned earlier, the adoption of a new strategy can lead to a rivalry between the legacy employees and the employees brought in to support the new strategy. This rivalry is the worst-case scenario and can be largely managed through clear vision and effective communication by the chief executive. If the new strategy is truly complementary and well defined, then communicating the advantages of effective teamwork and collaboration can insert energy into an organization even during times of transition. However, if the chief executive either cannot or will not communicate the vision, then instead of a complementary relationship, employees can see the new strategy as a competitor for internal resources. Once this mindset is established, it is very difficult to reverse.

While Strategic Expansion can provide significant growth opportunities, it adds complexity and obstacles to Talent Development. Depending on the strategy an organization chooses, Strategic Expansion not only requires a new set of capabilities, but it can also be significantly disruptive to personnel. For this reason, the leadership team must ensure that the Discipline of Talent Development is well established.

Wrapping Up

Most staffing companies struggle with the hiring, development, and retention of employees. Staffing is a demanding business that requires people to challenge themselves both personally and professionally. While you may invest a lot of time and money into your internal talent, it is important to keep in mind that Talent Development does not occur in a silo. Instead, the Discipline of Talent Development is mutually dependent on the other disciplines to have its intended impact.

The Discipline of Commitment provides an important narrative to internal talent, forming a foundation for a shared purpose by answering the question "Why?" The Discipline of Direction answers the questions

"What does this company do?" and "What makes it different from the competitors?" The Discipline of Culture creates the informal rules of behavior by establishing a shared belief system and defining expectations for everyone to embrace and reinforce. The health of each of these disciplines directly impacts Talent Development. If all the disciplines are strong, then it will be accelerated. However, if any of them is weak, Talent Development will be compromised.

Leaders who can effectively delegate the assessment, hiring, coaching, and motivation of their teams have taken one of the most difficult steps in building a self-sufficient, high-growth organization. All four areas of Talent Development are difficult to master yet crucial to the ongoing success of the company and represent the most common bottlenecks to growth.

Regardless of how well you hire and develop your personnel, this alone is not enough to ensure success. You also must enable your team to be successful by providing the necessary structure to allow individuals to maximize their potential and allow teams to collaborate effectively together. The role of this structure in breaking through will be discussed in the next chapter.

SUCCESS FACTORS FOR BREAKING THROUGH
THE DISCIPLINE OF TALENT DEVELOPMENT

Figure 6.1

Transition	Talent Development
Building an Independent Operation	Hire line-level managers to tackle day-to-day workflow and tactical firefighting. Delegate training, performance management, and hiring. Stay engaged with the team to assist with motivation but to also provide guidance on the assessment, promotion, and termination of personnel.
Achieving Organic Scale	Ensure there is a consistent performance management approach in place. Promote from within, if possible, to help ensure consistency. Focus on developing the autonomy of line-level managers, gradually increasing the scope of decision making while providing oversight. Conduct consistent management meetings to enable collaboration and brainstorming between managers.
Expanding Your Strategy	If the strategy is significantly different, be prepared to hire an executive who is a specialist in the field. Be willing to challenge bias on how roles need to be defined based on the legacy strategy. Assess, hire, and coach each role based on the strategy's unique needs. Focus on your professional development by educating yourself on the new strategy, attending industry events, and forming an advisory board.

Chapter 7:
The Discipline of Execution

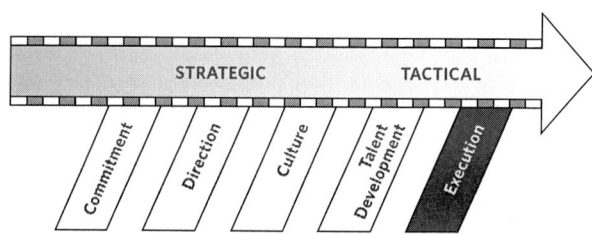

If you don't know how to execute, the whole of your effort as a leader will always be less than the sum of its parts.
—Ram Charan[36]

When Jake was hired for the Branch Manager role, it was made clear to him that he was inheriting a dysfunctional team. From his understanding, this dysfunction was a relatively recent phenomenon. Until recently, the Dallas office had been the top-performing branch, had most of the contest winners, and was considered the crown jewel of the company. When he asked his new employer what caused this rapid downward spiral, he never really got a clear answer. While the decline began with the loss of their largest account, it was employee morale that seemed to be the biggest issue. Sure there was complaining about specific employees, but Jake found it hard to believe that the decline was due to the attitude of a few employees.

On his first day, he could sense that something was not quite right. The branch felt more like a physician's waiting room than a $30 million IT staffing branch. At their first meeting, when he was introduced to the team, half of them were looking at the table, waiting for the meeting to end so they could get on to more important things. What Jake found peculiar was that those more important things did not seem to involve work. Every time he would walk by the cubes, there were people having discussions that had little to do with closing new business, instead focused on the latest office gossip. In addition, the few top performers dominated the attention of the rest of the team, creating cliques and dividing the culture.

Employee dissatisfaction was rampant. Jake spent the majority of the first few days taking complaints from employees and trying to distill down exactly what was driving this dysfunction. Over the next few weeks, he did notice there were some employees who contributed to the chaos, but he knew there was something else that was undermining the branch. Then he figured it out: Much of the branch operations were built around the account they lost just three months earlier, and all the weaknesses that were being overlooked were now front and center. Not only had they lost the account, but they did not know how to work together without it. There was no structure to build on.

There was no agreed upon workflow and no shared understanding of how to work together, thus creating cracks that would later be exploited by the more aggressive employees. The tools were dated, adding to the frustration as employees wasted their time double-documenting their work. Sales had their favorite recruiters, and certain recruiters chose not to work with certain salespeople. Candidates were kept in mailboxes and on Excel spreadsheets so as not to be stolen by peers. The lack of structure made the team not trust one another, spreading dysfunction among the formerly top-performing team.

It took nine months before the branch became healthy again. Some people had to be terminated, but not nearly the number that was initially speculated. New processes, policies, and tools transformed not just individual desks but also how the team worked with one another. There was still conflict, but it was largely productive conflict, not the type that paralyzed the branch earlier. It did not hurt that Jake had a much closer pulse on the branch by managing the day-to-day workflow as well as having the data to make the right decisions.

This scenario is fictional but very real, and it captures what can happen to an organization that has not defined the competitive practices necessary to drive daily workflow of their teams. As seen in the previous chapter, the Discipline of Talent Development ensures that organizations have the right people in the right roles and that they are properly trained to do their jobs. In this chapter, the Discipline of Execution focuses on establishing and managing to competitive practices that keep the organization running smoothly, even as it grows or experiences times of disruption.

There are three different types of essential practices: universal, industry specific, and competitive. Universal practices are general business practices that all businesses should follow. These practices are largely driven by compliance to government regulations and tax policy. They primarily reside in the back-office organization.

Industry specific practices are specific to an industry vertical but do not provide a unique competitive advantage. These practices include both front-office and back-office procedures that are required to meet the minimum service expectations of both clients and consultants. Examples of industry practices are accurate invoicing and payroll.

While companies have similar universal and industry specific practices, competitive practices vary widely from company to company. This is because competitive practices are the unique techniques a company leverages as differentiators to win market share. The Discipline of Execution specifically focuses on implementing processes, policies, and systems to ensure competitive practices are consistently executed within the sales and recruiting organization.

The impact of well-crafted competitive practices that are implemented properly should not be underestimated. Organizations with established competitive practices provide structure to their employees, which provides clarity and a natural momentum to their roles. They quickly learn how to succeed within the organization, collaborate more effectively with their peers, and have relatively few internal obstacles to their success. Organizations that do not have well-defined competitive practices create a "sink or swim" environment where only a small percentage of employees can be successful. An appropriate metaphor may be comparing a ballroom waltz with a mosh pit. One is well coordinated, allowing a large group of people to work in unison, while the other is individuals crashing into one another.

The temptation for leaders is to copy competitive practices from other staffing firms. While copying universal or industry specific practices may prove beneficial, replicating competitive practices is much more complicated. This complication is driven by the need for competitive practices to be in alignment with the other leadership disciplines. How teams conduct their jobs on a day-to-day basis is influenced by Commitment, Direction, Culture, and Talent.

The genius of many top-performing staffing firms is that their practices are easy to understand but difficult to replicate because they are part of a larger system of leadership disciplines. The balance of this chapter will explore how competitive practices should be developed to ensure proper alignment, examples of how they vary in both sales and recruiting, and how they evolve through the different phases of growth.

Ensuring Proper Alignment

The impact and scalability of competitive practices are dependent on how well they are aligned with all the leadership disciplines. Organizations that have strong alignment provide clarity throughout the organization, while ones that do not are constantly fighting internal contradictions that distract and confuse their teams. The answers to the following questions further clarify the relationships between alignment and execution of competitive practices. Think about these in relation to your organization.

Are the competitive practices consistent with the shared purpose or vision of the organization?

As we discussed in Chapter 1, the Discipline of Commitment is driven by answering the question "Why?" Commitment drives a shared purpose within the organization, justifying individual sacrifice and bolstering team collaboration. For this reason, competitive practices must not contradict the shared purpose or vision of the company. For example, if part of the shared purpose is to be a service focused organization but practices that treat contractors as a commodity are implemented, then there is an internal contradiction that impacts the entire organization. This contradiction undermines the execution of the competitive practices because employees sense that "it is not right." It also weakens commitment, as employees struggle with the hypocrisy of what the company says it is versus how it behaves.

Do the competitive practices drive the execution of the strategy?

Without proper execution, a strategy is as useful as daydreaming. The Discipline of Execution is what makes the strategy a reality and determines success or failure. With the potential exception of some of the developments in online staffing, there is no "blue ocean strategy" in staffing, where outthinking the competition leads to wide-scale disruption and increased market share. Staffing is a red ocean, a hypercompetitive industry where growth requires focused execution.[37] The company strategy provides that focus and must determine what competitive practices should be implemented. For instance, a transactional firm that does not streamline workflows to drive speed and submission volume will not be able to compete effectively. At a very tactical level, competitive practices must be implemented to bring the strategy to fruition; likewise, the strategy largely defines competitive practices a company needs.

Will the culture reinforce the behaviors needed to adhere to the competitive practices?

Reinforcing behavior at a peer-to-peer level is a central part of a Performance-Driven Culture, and this holds true with the consistent adherence to competitive practices as well. Competitive practices are the agreed upon workflows that influence how individuals run their desks as well as how they collaborate with peers. It is this predictability that builds trust within the team. If a recruiter knows that a salesperson has qualified a job based on certain standards, or if a salesperson knows that a candidate is properly prepped for the interview, then potential problems are minimized.

However, if competitive practices are not consistent with the company culture, employees are unlikely to follow them consistently, much less advocate for their enforcement. In some cases, the opposite can occur, where employees disagree with the practice. In these cases, employees have an unspoken agreement that they will not adhere to the practice, thus undermining its adoption. They do not see this as undermining the company—far from it. Instead, they see themselves as the company's immune system, eliminating threats that will hurt the company long-term. It is a mistake to underestimate the link between practices and culture. They work together to drive employee behavior. The more the two contradict one another the weaker both become.

Are the management and production teams capable of consistently adopting the practices?

Many companies attempt to implement competitive practices that their team simply does not have the experience or knowledge to execute. This is a common occurrence when staffing companies attempt to move up the value chain with additional offerings using the same personnel. One example is adding deliverable based services. This move to deliverables is most common in the IT space, where pursuing Statement of Work (SOW) or solutions business is an effective way to work around MSP/VMS programs. These offerings allow firms to work directly with managers and close higher-margin business. The challenge is that selling true SOW work is very different than selling staffing. Selling SOW work requires practices that can drive a longer sales cycle and incorporate subject matter experts. Also, multiple buyers can be involved, which adds to the complexity.

Adding SOW business is also often seen as benefiting the salesperson, because they now have "more arrows in the quiver" to sell to the client. This may be true for a small minority of versatile salespeople. However, for others, the addition of the service offering forces them to master another set of practices, which complicates their desk and leads to greater confusion as well as poor adoption. It will also distract them from the practices they need to master just to run an efficient staffing desk. While it can be done, companies have invested hundreds of thousands of dollars retraining their teams and hiring experts to expand into other service offerings only to realize that their sales team is unable to adopt the practices necessary to sell the new offerings.

Alignment with all the leadership disciplines is necessary for competitive practices to be adopted and scaled. It is also the alignment that truly drives the competitive practices that differentiate them from other firms. The high-performing staffing firms we studied have this alignment to a remarkable degree. In the next section, we will discuss in greater detail the role that competitive practices have in both sales and delivery as well as how they are developed.

Competitive Sales Practices

Since many staffing companies are founded by naturally strong salespeople, they tend to undervalue the importance of having well-defined sales practices. After all, the founders were able to be successful without them, so the need for them can seem counterintuitive. While there are examples of processes that are overly burdensome and of limited value, most successful salespeople can recognize that competitive practices provide important guidance and structure they need to be successful. It is also important to keep in mind the natural tension between structure and the need for individualism of the typical salesperson.

Salespeople like to set their own course and control their success. This is a common motivator that supplies many salespeople the energy and aggressiveness necessary in their role. Success in their role reflects individual accomplishment. It represents winning. When enforcing competitive practices through a sales process, it is important to take the power of individualism into account along with the experience and temperament of the sales team you need.

The whole purpose of a sales process is to ensure the consistent execution of competitive practices as well as avoiding conflict between employees. The process becomes a burden when it weakens motivation or eliminates innovative thinking from the role. We will address balancing structure and innovation in the "Breaking Through" section of this chapter.

This chapter is not meant to recommend one set of competitive practices or provide an encyclopedia of all the competitive practices in the industry. Instead, the focus will be on the nature of competitive practices and providing insight into how you can create your own. Developing competitive practices for the sales organization begins with a clearly defined sales strategy that answers the following questions:

- Who do we serve?
- What problems are we solving for them?
- How do we engage them?

The answers to these, of course, are your customers, your value proposition, and your competitive practices. To answer the question of how to bring these practices to life, it is useful to implement measurable objectives to distill down the critical capabilities required for effective client engagement. Remember from Chapter 6, objectives are measurable deliverables that are central to effective execution. The difference between the two sets of objectives is that sales objectives capture success factors for the entire sales organization instead of an individual role. But what should these objectives be based on? Most sales objectives are based on small and medium-sized business (SMB) development, account penetration, and staffing program business development.

Keep in mind that objectives only represent the end goal; the real question is, what sales practices allow those goals to be met? Based on these variables, it is easy to see how practices can vary so widely from company to company. To show how objectives translate into competitive practices, we will compare how practices are developed within SMB business development versus account penetration.

SMALL/MEDIUM BUYER

The small and medium-sized business (SMB) sales strategy targets the direct hiring manager who is not associated with any type of staffing program. Working with these buyers allows staffing companies to achieve better margins and close rates, primarily by using customer intimacy as the competitive differentiator. This intimacy provides a competitive advantage, giving the salesperson greater insight into job requirements and, in some cases, greater control over the hiring process. For these reasons, SMB sales strategy is typically associated with the Consultative Staffing Niche discussed in Chapter 4.

It is easy to assume that fast-growing staffing companies rely on enterprise accounts to drive their growth. This is not universally true. Many of them focus on SMB business as a central part of their strategy, as Tom Gimbel of LaSalle Network discusses.

Focusing on the smaller volume users has been key for us. I would rather have a hundred clients with just one temp than one client using a hundred temps. When you look for the small volume users, you will end up finding the big volume users.

With the high transaction volume, we have strong metrics on meetings attended, new meetings with different hiring managers, and then cross-selling. For the first three to five years, our new salespeople are very focused on new client acquisition. Our more tenured people are looking for the larger accounts.

—Tom Gimbel, LaSalle Network

The goal of diversification is obvious. Diversification and profitability are the main benefits of the SMB strategy. Tom also outlines that small volume users will lead to high volume users. This may seem to be a contradiction, but the fundamental point is that the more people you do business with the more likely you will be associated with people who move to a larger organization or their current organization experiences rapid growth either organically or through a merger. This point touches on a fundamental truth: The more relationships you have the "luckier" you will become.

The Achilles' heel of the SMB sales strategy is consistent job order volume, which requires a highly aggressive sales organization. The objective in this case is to increase job order volume. If diversification is an additional area of focus, the objective may be to increase job order volume from new accounts. For the purposes of this discussion, we will assume the latter.

Growth and diversification within the SMB strategy is more than just hiring hunters; it is about building an organization that can enable those hunters to be successful. Great companies build competitive practices so they do not have to hire the top 5% of sales talent. Instead, they build competitive practices that enable a broader range of people to be successful in the role.

For the SMB sales strategy, the most common competitive practice is lead generation. Leads can range from identifying specific hiring needs at new prospects to business intelligence focusing on general information, such as overall contractor usage. Many lead generation programs come in the form of lead blitzes. A lead blitz focuses the team on generating leads over a short period of time. Short-term lead blitzes are an effective way to temporarily boost business development activity, though the large influx of leads can overwhelm the sales team and negatively impact their ability to convert those leads into business. In addition, lead blitzes can only be done sporadically because they lose their effectiveness after they become a "business as usual" activity.

Staffing firms with a strong SMB sales strategy do not depend on lead blitzes but instead have incorporated lead generation as part of their standard workflow. These firms understand that their recruiters have leads in front of them daily and need to establish the habit of asking the right questions. But identifying leads is only half the equation; the other half is ensuring effective follow-up from the sales team. Witnessing firms with strong programs made it is easy to attribute their disciplined approach to leads as cultural, though we would argue that there is a codependent relationship between culture and competitive practices. Changes in one will always affect the other.

LEAD GENERATION PROGRAM METRICS

Figure 7.1

Metric	Personnel	Purpose
Number of Leads	Recruiting	This metric measures the ability of the recruiter to extract leads from their conversations with candidates. It is critical not to conflate with leads from job boards or other sources since those leads are unqualified and will undermine the effectiveness of the program. For that reason, it is better to keep the number of leads lower and focus on quality.
Number of Meetings from Leads or Percent of Leads Converted to Meetings	Sales and Recruiting	This is a measure primarily to ensure effective lead follow-up by sales. At the same time, it can be a measure of lead quality from the recruiter.
Number of Job Orders from Leads or Percent of Leads Converted to Job Orders	Sales	Further downstream, metrics indirectly measure follow-up as well as salesperson's ability to capture the job order. These metrics are not ideal for measuring the quality of the lead itself unless there is a high level of confidence that sales is executing properly.
Number of Placements from Leads or Percent of Placements Converted from Leads	Sales	Furthest downstream, this metric reflects sales as well as the ultimate effectiveness of the program as a whole.

Governing a lead generation program requires that management drive team behavior through a combination of metrics and workflow management. By leveraging these tools, management can drive lead generation as well as measuring lead quality and sales follow-up. Figure 7.1 details some common metrics that can be used to provide the initial framework of a lead generation program.

The competitive practice of lead generation is a common one in the industry. But developing it as a consistent competitive practice requires well-defined objectives and measures that are then use to embed the behavior as part of the normal day-to-day operations. To reinforce how competitive practices vary, we will now consider a different sales strategy of account penetration and management.

ACCOUNT PENETRATION AND MANAGEMENT

Just as new business development is critical for diversification, account penetration is the primary driver for growth in many companies. Developing the right objectives for this strategy may be something as simple as increasing revenue at enterprise accounts. Of course, you need to define an enterprise account, and for most companies when they reach a certain size, the term becomes unwieldly. But for Cindy Pasky of Strategic Staffing Solutions, whose massive growth was driven by just over 20 enterprise accounts, her objectives were much more aggressive.

———◇———

To really penetrate a large account, you have to be number one in multiple categories. You have to be number one in compliance, number one in performance based on how they measure it, and then number one not necessarily in size but in perception of relationship. If you are too small, it does not matter how you did in those other things; it is too easy to get rid of you. But if you are in those top three from a size standpoint but number one in the other areas, nothing is ever a given and you have to earn it every day, but you really reduce the chances that you will not be carried forward, even if there is an acquisition or a merger or a downturn.

—Cindy Pasky, Strategic Staffing Solutions

Cindy runs a highly disciplined organization that focuses not only on growth but is also hypervigilant on complying with the regulations and back-office requirements of the staffing programs they support. She knew that her company needed to be trusted from all parts of the organization for the relationship not only to be stable but to thrive. The nature of enterprise accounts is that the more business an account provides you, the greater the risk to your company as your reliance on them increases. Managing account penetration is not just about growth; it is about mitigating risk. While enterprise accounts can drive rapid growth, they can also turn on a dime with a single phone call and put massive amounts of gross profit at risk. Cindy's philosophy on growth and risk management at enterprise accounts could be its own book, given the complexity and business at stake in these large accounts.

For our purposes when talking about account penetration and management, we will focus on two objectives that are similar to the ones we addressed in the SMB section: growth and diversification. Our objective for this exercise will be to improve penetration at enterprise accounts.

With the SMB sales strategy, we focused on lead generation as a common competitive practice. Lead generation is a competitive practice that lends itself to a linear and somewhat predictable workflow that can be measured in a variety of ways: A recruiter identifies a lead; the lead is assigned; the salesperson follows up; and there is a positive or negative result. However, not all competitive practices are driven through a linear process; some rely more on collaboration and creative problem solving.

The competitive practice of account planning enables a more creative approach to selling. As seen in Figures 7.2 and 7.3, managing this competitive practice is not just about the amount of activity but also leveraging all activity as a means to create a stronger working relationship and, therefore, strategic advantage at the account.

Account planning improves the understanding of the client's organizational structure as well as business initiatives that drive contingent labor spend. This knowledge allows sales to penetrate the account more effectively in a couple ways. First, it provides a roadmap of where sales and management need to focus their time, making meeting activity and joint sales calls much more productive. Second, it increases the credibility of the sales team as they use their in-depth knowledge of the account to differentiate themselves in meetings.

Another strategic advantage of account planning is developing trusting relationships with senior-level decision makers. A client's Human Resources or Procurement professionals often have influence over the scope of the business a staffing company is approved to support, not to mention whether the staffing company stays on as a vendor. In addition, these buyers can provide insight into future projects and support the staffing company if it finds itself at risk.

It is important to keep in mind that not only do the motivations of key decision makers often vary from line-level buyers, but they also can quickly change without notice. Having strong communication lines with the strategic decision makers protects the staffing company from losing the client but can also provide the opportunity to become a trusted advisor regarding the state of the program, which can lead to growth possibilities.

ACCOUNT PLANNING METRICS

Figure 7.2

Metrics	Purpose
Number of Meetings with New Managers Number of Total Meetings	For most organizations, meetings represent the most important activity metric in sales. Account Managers can fall into the trap of meeting the same group of managers multiple times to hit their activity goal. Adding meetings with new managers avoids this work-around.
Number of Job Orders Received Before the Competition	Time is a competitive differentiator that allows recruiters to reach out to the candidate market before the competition. A salesperson who is able to work a qualified job before the competition is one that is well networked in the organization and has been able to establish trusting relationships with hiring managers.
Submittal-to-Hire Ratio	The best measure of productivity for an account manager, this measure not only captures the ability to qualify jobs, but it also reveals influence throughout the buying process over both the client and the recruiting team.
Job Order Close Rate	This is a common but tricky measure since it is directly impacted by variations on job order volume. However, when trend analysis over time normalizes, that variability makes it a relevant measure.

To evaluate the activity in account management, metrics are certainly important, but an account plan looks beyond metrics. While you can set meeting goals for a salesperson, it is necessary to understand that not all meetings are created equal. Complementing the activity metrics with specific targets within the account helps ensure that meetings are occurring to help with the long-term penetration of the account. Figures 7.2 and 7.3 give examples of how a combination of metrics and tasks can be used to drive the competitive practice of account planning.

ACCOUNT PLANNING TASKS

Figure 7.3

Tasks	Purpose
Support charity event sponsored by xyz client.	Solidify relationships with key decision makers and create opportunities to meet new contacts at the event. Often, clients will ask vendors to sponsor events; however, it is much more impactful when the initiative comes from the vendor.
Schedule a joint meeting or golf outing with the VP of Infrastructure.	This VP is a senior decision maker who is typically off the salesperson's radar since they do not hire contractors directly. The manager, in this case, realizes that there is a lack of traction in this group and sees the opportunity to gain some leverage and strategic insight by developing a relationship with this VP.
Schedule a health check with the program manager to review performance.	While many staffing programs conduct frequent reviews, many do not until they are evaluating their vendors. In this case, the manager is unsure how they are lining up against the competition. This meeting has the added benefit of strengthening the relationship with the program manager, potentially leading to important intelligence regarding the state of the program.

Successful account planning is not for just historical reference; instead, it provides tactical and strategic guidance to the account manager to improve account penetration. This contrasts with lead generation, which is more process driven. Both of these examples provide insight into the variety of competitive practices that can be implemented and how they affect employee performance differently.

When it comes to executing sales strategies, top-performing staffing firms understand that they must make their sales organization a priority for their organization to survive. For sales to be effective, it must be intentionally proactive, creating opportunity that normally would not exist or seeing opportunities before the competition. This leaves sales much more vulnerable and dependent on well-designed practices to ensure effective execution of the sales strategies they are pursuing.

Most significantly, the ability to control the long-term direction of a staffing firm is directly dependent on the health of the sales organization. A company with a strong sales organization can pick and choose what clients to support, while one with a weak sales organization becomes more and more dependent on legacy accounts. Therefore, understanding how to manage practices for each of the sales strategies is critical not only for short-term production but for the long-term growth and independence of the staffing company. Regardless of the strength of the sales organization, it is only as good as the ability to deliver.

Competitive Delivery Practices

Competitive delivery practices focus on ensuring that delivery capabilities are aligned with the success factors of your clients. Unlike sales, recruiting lends itself to predictable linear workflows that can be tightly defined. This makes competitive practices much more process focused than typically seen in sales. While most of this section will focus on recruiting, the role of the sales team must also be considered. This is to avoid the common mistakes of categorizing competitive practices only by employee role and leaving out practices that focus on collaboration.

DELIVERY SUCCESS FACTORS

Figure 7.4

Competitive Strategy	Delivery Success Factors
Transactional Staffing	• Speed and price are primary differentiators • Little-to-no sales involvement • Streamlined processes • Low cost per submittal • Quick response time • Automated sourcing • Offshore recruiting/hybrid onshore/offshore
Consultative Staffing	• Service quality is the primary differentiator • Sales strives for customer intimacy • Sales acts as quality control for delivery • Processes focus on collaboration over speed
High Demand Niche Staffing	• Niche talent is primary differentiator • Sales skill markets talent • Proactive candidate pipelining is key recruiting discipline • Processes focus on collaboration • Speed and quality are achieved by niche focus
Deliverable Based Staffing	• Service scope is the primary differentiator • Sales must be able to develop and sell solutions • Collaborate with subject matter experts (SMEs) in selling service • Recruiting can be a mix of proactive and reactive sourcing • SMEs conduct final qualification

Achieving alignment begins with the success factors of the competitive strategy a company chooses to pursue. Different strategies require different delivery capabilities. Figure 7.4 provides examples of what recruiting effectiveness may look like for each strategy. This is not meant to capture all the differences but instead shows a contrast into how recruiting effectiveness needs to be influenced by the niche that its company services.

Within each competitive strategy, there are three delivery capabilities to evaluate: speed, submittal throughput, and quality. When developing competitive practices, all three must be considered with the goal of achieving the right balance that best matches the strategy. When it comes to competitive practices, it is important to realize that an effective practice supporting one strategy can be a significant liability in another. To highlight this distinction, let us look at each of these in more depth.

Speed

Speed is a competitive necessity for transactional staffing firms, but it also plays an important role for both consultative and niche-based firms. In the process and data-driven world of transactional staffing, there is very little time to pause and consider the best approach to a job order. Instead, the approach is to react quickly with candidates and wait for feedback. The focus on speed reduces candidate quality, but transactional firms are about speed first, cost second, and quality third. Buyers in this niche are simply looking for a "good enough" candidate fast.

In contrast, speed is the Achilles' heel for the consultative staffing company, sometimes resulting in poor communication and ineffective submittals that could damage the client relationship. Without the predictability of the niche-based firm and competitive practices that focus on collaboration over efficiency, speed provides a significant challenge.

This especially poses a problem when the consultative staffing firm veers outside their strategy. Often, these consultative firms are thrust into the transactional space by a client and are given little choice but to either support the client or lose a substantial portion of its business.

Submittal Throughput

Submittal throughput is another major capability that staffing firms consider when developing competitive practices. Submittal throughput is primarily a measure of the volume of submissions a recruiting team can efficiently generate. However, submittal throughput is not just about the volume of candidates an organization can generate; it is also about ensuring a proper financial return. Achieving this return varies based on the strategy a staffing firm chooses with transactional clients, providing the greatest ROI challenges.

Transactional clients tend to challenge ROI in two ways. First is by gross margin pressure. This pressure can be applied either by lowering the bill rate or through rebates, such as volume discounts or prompt-pay discounts. The second challenge to ROI is the recruiting costs required to support these programs. The cost is primarily driven by high submittal-to-hire ratios. These ratios are driven up by the competitiveness of the business and can be made worse by Service Level Agreements (SLAs) required by the client. All these factors force staffing firms to bring down the cost of submittals to remain profitable.

Competitive practices can reduce cost in one of two ways. They can decrease the cost per submittal and/or improve the submittal-to-hire ratio. Decreasing the cost per submission has led many staffing firms to build offshore recruiting centers. Due to lower cost of labor, this allows their costs per submission to be a fraction of other firms as well as generating the submittal volume needed to support the account effectively. On the flip side, this can negatively impact quality, further highlighting the trade-offs executives must be willing to make when building delivery capabilities.

Other competitive practices control costs through reducing submittal-to-hire ratios, which relies on having access to the hiring manager to influence the buying process. This approach runs in contrast to the rules of engagement for many staffing programs. Many consultative and niche staffing firms choose this because restructuring the recruiting organization is disruptive and can undermine the other parts of the business. Instead, these firms leverage their expertise and service quality to justify higher rates and tend to be more selective on the job orders they decide to work.

Quality

If you ask most clients what is important to them, they typically stress candidate quality. SIA's survey of large buyers has consistently shown over the years that buyers claim candidate quality as their top consideration when choosing a staffing supplier.[38] A recent survey found that 53% of buyers saw candidate quality as the criteria for choosing a staffing supplier. The trick for the quality-driven staffing firm is to work with the companies that actually mean it. We live in a data-driven world where efficiency and cost reduction are often seen as unstoppable trends. The quality-driven firm holds the more traditional view that staffing is fundamentally a people driven industry. That is not to say that they do not look for efficiencies or try to get faster; it just means that those things are secondary to a more intimate, customer service oriented model.

Developing competitive practices supporting this model comes at a cost. For the consultative staffing firms, these costs often come in the form of the local branches. The upfront costs of opening a branch and making it profitable as well as the additional leadership head count can be extensive. For the niche firms, the costs may not be in branches but instead in keeping high demand talent on the bench between gaps in assignment. For the delivery-based firm, they may have the cost of a local presence in addition to the cost of subject matter experts who are required to both sell and deliver the projects.

Another significant cost for the quality-driven firm is the investment in sales. Unlike a transactional firm that typically does not need to hunt down job orders, the quality-driven firm needs a strong sales organization to continuously identify new opportunities.

The reason these high-cost models can work, as proven by some of the top-performing staffing firms, is that there is a strong market for quality. There are buyers willing to pay relatively well for the service and willing to work closely with the staffing company. This closer collaboration with the buyers typically leads to higher margins along with strong close rates and submittal-to-hire ratios, which pay for the higher upfront cost.

Speed, submittal throughput, and quality are necessary in every delivery organization. However, when it comes to competitive practices, it is about where a staffing executive is going to focus their differentiation. Transactional firms must produce a large volume of candidates quickly, and thus, they must build operations that are lean and efficient. For quality-driven firms, the ability to be intimately involved and adaptable to meet the client's needs requires an operation that prioritizes collaboration and creative problem solving over efficiency.

As mentioned earlier, competitive practices in delivery are typically woven into day-to-day processes. For further clarification, the next section will give examples of how competitive practices within job order management, sourcing, and submittal management can impact delivery capabilities.

Job Order Management: Job Order Qualification, Prioritization, and Assignment

Job order management represents the most important competitive practice within the delivery organization: Which job orders an organization decides to work influence every other aspect of delivery. If an organization is inefficient in managing its jobs, it cannot compete on speed, just as an organization that does not qualify job orders cannot focus on quality. Nothing can be done with sourcing or submittal management to rectify any weaknesses in job order management. Next we will discuss critical practices within job order management that enable speed, submittal throughput, and quality.

<u>Speed</u>: The time it takes for recruiters to begin sourcing on a job order once it hits the market represents one of the biggest sources of delays in the speed-driven firm. The cause of these delays can be an intermediary, most commonly a "salesperson," who receives the job from the portal and then must release it to the recruiting team. As was mentioned in the previous chapter, a salesperson in this role is a poor utilization of resources, especially if they cannot influence the buying process. When speed is a crucial success factor, a lean delivery structure should remove obstacles to allow a recruiter to begin sourcing on the job immediately.

Another effective competitive practice that can assist with speed is the timely removal of jobs out of the active queue after a designated period of time. Too often, firms keep a job open even though they know it is too late to respond to it. These jobs act as a distraction and, if not managed properly, can impact responsiveness to new jobs. Effective job order management is about playing the odds. The cleaner the job order queue the more efficient the team will be.

Submittal Throughput: Job order management's impact on submittal volume is relatively limited in comparison to speed and quality. However, submittal volume can be impacted by methods that are effectively opposite of one another. The first method is to create a laissez-faire environment where all the recruiters can work on any job they choose and with very limited candidate ownership. This requires all recruiters to have visibility to all the jobs simultaneously with no restrictions on what they choose to work. The other method is to assign jobs based on predictable skill sets and/or accounts. By focusing recruiters either by skill sets or accounts, it decreases the variability of the job orders that they work on, allowing them to build networks and become more effective in covering more jobs.

Quality: How job orders are qualified before they reach the recruiting team is a foundational competitive practice for a quality-driven firm, and arguably the most important. A well-qualified job order impacts all the processes that are downstream from it, including how candidates are sourced, qualified, and presented to the client. The less qualified a job order is the less impact the other quality-driven processes have. It is for this reason that a poorly qualified job has an inordinate negative impact on the quality-driven firm, especially compared to the transactional firm. Quality depends largely on effective collaboration between the client, sales, and recruiting team, and many firms with these models assign recruiters to specific salespeople or accounts. This allows teams to become more familiar with each other, improving communication.

Sourcing: Candidate Identification and Qualification

Once competitive practices for job order management have been defined, a company must focus on the competitive practices for sourcing. How an organization identifies and qualifies talent determines the candidate pools they can effectively use, and this largely determines the type of clients they can support. The competitive practice of sourcing provides an important competitive differentiator, especially in tight labor markets. Balancing speed, submittal throughput, and quality places a significant role in how candidates are presented to clients and whether that approach meets clients' expectations.

Speed: Unless there is the ability to place proactively pipelined candidates, sourcing for speed-based firms relies on readily available talent, primarily from internet job boards, social media, and their proprietary database. For that reason, these firms should be willing to invest in job boards and aggregators as well as the ability to search and send mass communications from their proprietary database. While these competitive practices can take away from developing loyal connections with candidates, it achieves the primary goal of finding talent that is actively looking very quickly and very efficiently. In addition, candidate qualification must also be streamlined to speed up the candidate's submission to the client. In this case, recruiters should be trained to effectively screen candidates over the phone to get the submission to the client as quickly as possible.

Submittal Throughput: Building competitive practices that enable submittal throughput are attempting to accomplish two things: deliver a large volume of submittals and do so with a low per-unit cost. Firms that rely on cheap submittals to counteract high submittal-to-hire ratios must also rely on job boards and mass communication. In addition, many firms invest in sourcers. Sourcers are responsible for the identification of the resumes but typically do not qualify the candidates. For repeatable skills sets, sourcers can be effective. Where sourcers struggle is supporting a variety of high-level skill sets. This is especially true for IT staffing, where sourcing candidates requires a significant level of expertise in and of itself.

Quality: Quality-driven competitive practices invariably sacrifice both speed and submittal throughput. With a level of influence over the buying process and a greater level of job qualification, recruiters now have the time to be able to source and qualify high-quality candidates. This allows a recruiter to use more traditional methods, such as networking or tapping into passive candidate pools from proprietary databases or LinkedIn. Once the recruiter identifies a candidate, they then typically follow a more rigorous candidate qualification process than the firms that focus more on speed and submittal throughput. This may include in-person interviews, background checks, additional skill screening, and/or a final screening by the account executive. Quality firms also typically encourage creative problem solving between recruiting and sales. They will often present the client with other options that may be outside the scope of the original job order. Presenting these different options often clarifies the job further or opens solutions to the client that they did not initially consider.

Submittal Management: Candidate Submission, Client Interview, and Placement

How candidates are managed throughout the hiring process has important ramifications on a staffing firm's relationship with both clients and candidates. Submittal management is the process that includes all activities from sending the resume to the client to placing that candidate. Submittal management focuses on creating competitive practices that are efficient while, at the same time, maintaining the right level of intimacy.

Submittal management has the most time consuming competitive practices in delivery, but these practices largely define the relationship between the staffing firm and the people they are serving.

Speed: Just as reducing the time job orders are released to recruiters is a key success factor, so is the time it takes to get that submittal to the hands of the client. When measuring speed as a success factor, it is really measuring the time from when the job order is released to the marketplace up to when the candidate submission is made to the client. For that reason, competitive practices should seek to streamline the submission process. One of the most common approaches allows the recruiters to submit directly to the client for both local and offshore recruiters. For accounts where a salesperson cannot provide any value, this is an effective approach. However, one of the more common mistakes people make is hiring junior-level recruiters with minimal training to support those jobs to keep down the cost per submission. Without significant training or hiring experienced recruiters, this is a high risk, low return approach.

Submittal Throughput: Increasing submittal numbers requires that the vast majority of a recruiter's time is spent sourcing and qualifying candidates. In order to do this, the recruiter typically must limit the amount of time they spend managing the large volume of pending submissions they have in the queue. Because of this, ongoing communication with active submissions is often limited to when there is an interview request or other updates from the client. In some cases, candidates are not even notified when they are eliminated from consideration. For this reason, it is the desire for submittal volume that has such a negative impact on how staffing firms are perceived by candidates.

While it is easy to blame the staffing firms for poor communication, it is a predictable outcome of staffing programs that have high submittal-to-hire ratios driven by submittal KPIs and/or too many vendors. Any model that requires a low cost per submission to be successful is going to drive down the quality of the candidate and client experience. This opens up opportunity for new models, such as online staffing platforms, which can provide a better candidate experience with greater feelings of control over the process and more clear communication about the candidate's status.

Quality: For quality-driven firms, candidate loyalty is a key differentiator. Candidate loyalty reduces the margin for error during the submittal management process and can play a key role in a successful assignment once the candidate is placed. Establishing candidate loyalty begins with the first conversation and is solidified by the candidate experience throughout the submittal management process. Quality-driven firms contrast themselves with firms that focus on speed and submittal throughput by more in-depth conversations during initial sourcing calls followed up by consistent communication and support through the submittal management process. It is a more time consuming and intimate approach to submittal management but one that leads to better ratios and a higher level of service for both the candidate and client.

Competitive delivery practices in job order management, sourcing, and submittal management must properly balance speed, submittal throughput, and quality. This balance is achieved primarily through how processes are designed and aligned with one another. For a staffing firm that focuses on speed, all key processes must be streamlined. In a quality-focused firm, checks are implemented to ensure standards are being met. Both approaches represent trade-offs that the management team must intentionally design and enforce to ensure consistency and build a competitive delivery organization.

Chapter 7: The Discipline of Execution

Breaking Through: Innovate and Replicate

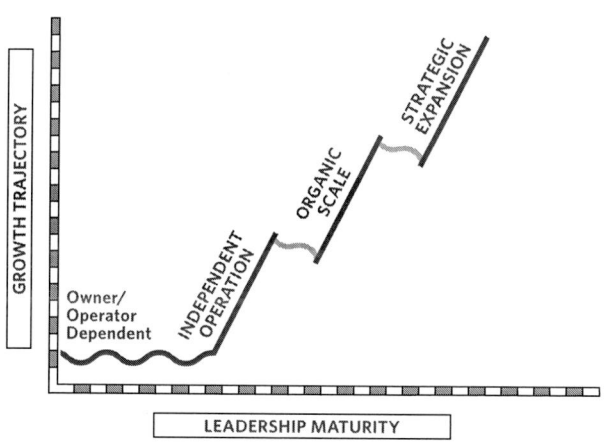

Competitive practices in sales and recruiting allow an organization to scale team performance through consistent and efficient execution. However, the structure that competitive practices provide must also be balanced with the need for innovation. Achieving this balance is crucial for an organization to break through.

To implement competitive practices in their organizations, management must leverage policies, processes, and tools.

- Policies are a set of principles that aid in defining appropriate behavior. This includes items such as compensation plans, candidate and account ownership policies, vacation, and required office hours.
- Processes are standardized workflows that determine how certain activity should be done. Common processes include how jobs and candidates are qualified as well as processes focusing on prospecting.
- Tools act as a catalyst to certain workflows and provide metrics and documentation for management to retain operational visibility. Some of these tools include applicant tracking systems, analytics, market research sites, job boards, and external resume banks.

Continuous improvement of policies, processes, and tools are crucial for a staffing company to remain competitive. Ron Shahani of Acro highlights the importance of continuous improvement.

Chapter 7: The Discipline of Execution

---○---

As Acro enjoyed rapid growth, we found that some existing processes could not meet the demands of increased scale. 'More of the same' became increasingly inefficient, and new processes had to be developed. Nearly all of the various processes involved in our business have been improved, streamlined, and automated by continual advancements in information technologies and Acro's ongoing development of software solutions.

—*Ron Shahani, Acro Service Corporation*

---○---

While it would be a fool's errand to attempt to capture how all competitive practices change through the different phases of growth, what can be done is providing insight into how practices become established and evolve.

Policies, processes, and tools enable competitive practices to become established through a combination of enablement and governance. Enablement creates momentum for the practice, so it is in the employee's best interest to follow it. Governance establishes practices through enforcement. In the end, competitive practices provide structure to the daily life of employees through a carrot-and-stick approach. However, in an entrepreneurial business like staffing, how much structure is enough, and when is it too much?

How leaders drive business on a day-to-day basis is largely defined by the size of the organization. For Owner/Operator Dependent firms, there is very little structure needed to drive performance since daily interaction typically suffices to keep the team aligned and focused. A strong argument can be made that during this phase, innovation and adaptability are an important competitive advantage. There are a couple reasons for this. First, since the Owner/Operator is so involved in the business, they have visibility into the behavior of employees, so governance can still be effective even if it is largely informal.

Second, the executive often needs to be flexible to attract employees. This includes policy flexibility in areas such as compensation plans. More importantly, however, the Owner/Operator phase is a testing ground. These professionals are testing the market's response to their strategies, which allows them to observe and modify different competitive practices until they find the ones that best meet the needs of their strategies and their management styles. In addition, at the Owner/Operator phase, the relative cost of innovation is low, but the return can be significant.

A common mistake for Owner/Operators is to try to skip this crucial step and instead simply copy practices they see the competition doing. However, as mentioned earlier, competitive practices must align with the other leadership disciplines, so attempting to simply replicate practices with a trial-and-error mentality is skipping over a crucial step in the company's development. The time to test different policies, processes, and to a lesser extent, tools is when change is easy to manage. Simply put, innovation should be the priority. Use this beginning phase to learn how you want to manage and what practices you want to implement. This requires more work, but it is nothing compared to the work needed to undo poorly conceived practices when the organization is larger and more difficult to adapt.

BUILDING AN INDEPENDENT OPERATION

While the Owner/Operator Dependent phase focuses on defining what competitive practices need to be implemented, the Independent Operation phase formalizes them. The first step toward this is by standardizing policies. Policies such as compensation plans often need to vary during the Owner/Operator phase to attract the right talent. However, as an organization becomes larger, these inconsistencies become less and less sustainable. While there still may be some inconsistencies, they need to be minimized to decrease or avoid disruption. The same is true for vacation policies and business hours. In the Owner/Operator phase, that flexibility can act as an attraction. However, as an organization grows, the lack of standardization begins to weaken accountability and interfere with team collaboration, undermining not only individual performance but the culture as a whole.

Depending on the market niche, sales and recruiting processes begin to play a role in the establishment of competitive practices. During the Owner/Operator phase, many chief executives are effective at providing ad hoc situational coaching to a small sales team. For an organization to become an Independent Operation, some of this coaching is often delegated to new management.

At the very minimum, a sales process should enable line-level management to manage sales territories and measure the progress within those territories. This allows the manager to ensure that the salesperson is focused on the right accounts and that they have the right amount of activity at those accounts. However, a sales process does have diminishing returns. A little process can provide the right amount of structure, but an overly burdensome one can eliminate initiative and creativity. Process cannot replace strong sales leadership, as it too often does.

As a general rule, choose the least structured process you can and ensure your sales leaders are involved in client meetings, not sitting in their offices creating sales funnels and Excel spreadsheets.

Implementation of delivery processes can be more aggressive during the Independent Operation phase, and the level of structure these processes provide is largely determined by the nature and volume of job orders. Independent Operations with high job order flow first need to focus on more upstream processes, such as how jobs are prioritized and assigned. Without rigor in this area, job order volume can wreak havoc on an Independent Operation, especially for organizations that have a transactional competitive strategy. Consultative staffing firms typically do not have these types of issues at the Independent Operation phase, so job order prioritization and assignment is less of a priority. Instead, these firms focus on competitive practices that strengthen job order and candidate qualification.

Tools also begin to play a greater role in both the enablement and governance of competitive practices. At this phase, it is not uncommon for executives to upgrade their applicant tracking systems and CRM. These tools not only provide functionality to make the sales and recruiting desks more productive, but they also provide data to the management team. Managing to data becomes more crucial as the chief executive becomes more removed from the day-to-day, and line-level managers must now manage personnel as well as daily processes. Data not only allows managers to manage a more complex operation, but it also becomes crucial for effective communication between members of the management team. Anecdotal evidence and gut feel can no longer govern the organization effectively. Managers now need real data to verify their assumptions and make better decisions.

Within the Independent Operation phase, competitive practices that have largely been defined must now be formalized through a combination of policies, processes, and tools. Consistency now becomes a larger priority, and innovation, while still important, must now be more measured as the operation becomes more complex and less adaptable to change. Toward the end of the Independent Operation phase, competitive practices are proven enough to be replicated and enable the company to achieve Organic Scale.

ACHIEVING ORGANIC SCALE

When it comes to execution, achieving Organic Scale relies on the effective replication of practices while still meeting the unique needs of individual markets. As a general rule, competitive practices that focus on desk level techniques should be replicated, as should the vast majority of policies. Other processes that focus on the unique challenges of a larger branch, such as job order prioritization, can be put aside. In many cases, strong local management can show enough discernment to determine what practices should be replicated and when.

The amount of autonomy on competitive practices to give local branch management is a significant decision and should not be taken lightly. Most talented leaders desire some level of autonomy, just like top-performing salespeople, while other leaders require well-defined competitive practices to give them parameters. In addition, it is not uncommon for innovation to come from remote branches, which often face a different set of challenges. These unique challenges will force them to develop competitive practices that not only meet the needs of their market but may benefit other branches as well. It is common for leaders to believe that most cutting edge improvements come from the home office; however, this bias can cause leaders to overlook substantial improvements that are occurring out in the field.

For firms that want their remote offices to have a level of autonomy to develop new competitive practices, they should consider the following cause-and-effect relationships:

1. *The further upstream you measure, the more control you are exerting over competitive practices.*

Executives who measure and manage to calls, screens, emails, and voicemails are sending a message that there is one best way to do things. This approach is fine, and many executives manage their teams that way. However, this approach tends to dampen innovation from line-level managers. Executives who want to give their managers more autonomy focus more on result metrics than activity metrics. Result metrics give managers the freedom to try different approaches, knowing that as long as they hit goal, the rest does not matter. Executives who want to prioritize standardization over innovation focus their attention on the how, which is the activity. Executives prioritizing innovation focus on the what, which is the results.

2. *Innovation requires collaboration to reach its full potential.*

Most firms have management meetings where line-level managers discuss the state of the operations with their peers and the executive team. In organizations that lean more toward standardization, these meetings are very metric focused, often comparing the performance of their operations to the various benchmarks provided by executive management. This is an effective way to reinforce the importance of these numbers. Firms wishing to focus on innovation will focus less on the upstream numbers and more on results and the new challenges and opportunities that market is facing. Much of the time can then be spent brainstorming different approaches, pulling from the experience of the entire management team.

3. *Innovation requires talent and experience.*

The more talented and experienced the line-level management team is, the less structure they need and, therefore, the more freedom they can have to innovate. However, inexperienced managers need structure, and the lure of innovation can be a significant distraction, leading them down the wrong road and negatively impacting production. In those cases, replication of tried-and-true competitive practices is the safest route.

4. *Tread carefully with innovation driven from corporate.*

Corporate shared services will have a tendency to cross over into driving innovation in competitive practices. This can work as long as the employees driving the improvements have recently worked in the business and understand what is happening in the branches. However, the tendency over time is for corporate shared services to get more and more isolated from the field, diminishing their understanding of the real challenges of the business. If not kept in check, they will roll out competitive practices that simply do not work or are not adopted in the field. As a general rule, these types of rollouts need to be reviewed with the utmost scrutiny.

Balancing innovation versus replication is an important part of achieving Organic Scale. As with all questions regarding competitive practices, there is no one right answer for all companies. Instead, leaders must decide on an approach based on the talent of the remote managers and the needs of their competitive strategy. While innovation is highly regarded by most business thought leaders, it is important to be aware of the potential risks when unqualified leaders are asked to think "outside the box" instead of following proven competitive practices.

EXPANDING YOUR STRATEGY

Once your competitive practices are well established and have been proven to be scalable, it may be appropriate to consider an additional strategy. This requires a clear understanding of the level of compatibility of competitive practices. Strategies with a high level of compatibility can leverage competitive practices and likely other operational strengths to minimize the level of distraction and shore up the new strategy as it begins to take form.

A strategy with a high level of compatibility may be for an IT staffing firm to open a finance and accounting (F&A) division. These two strategies often share senior-level buyers who require both F&A and IT resources. They are both professional staffing, so the sales and recruiting processes are more similar than different. The profitability and length of contract are also similar, making policies such as compensation plans relevant for both.

That is not to say an expansion such as this would be easy. There is still extensive training, branding, and investment in a leader who knows the business, knows how to build a start-up operation, and can effectively collaborate with employees and leaders of the legacy business. Considering these factors, it is easy to understand the complexity of even a relatively conservative expansion.

The less compatibility between the new strategy and the legacy strategy, the more dependent the organization is on the quality of the new leader to provide insight into the competitive practices that need to be developed. In addition, the new leader needs to balance the implementation of these new practices with the current culture and priorities of the legacy business.

This tension can often be seen when considering very tactical issues. For example, a firm decides to expand into the MSP space and hires a specialist to lead it. They now must build competitive practices, including new sales processes and governance. Having operational rigor is crucial since the legacy sales team will be reluctant to adopt new practices as well as transitioning their relationships to an unproven operation. This reluctance will not be overt; however, if not addressed, it will be enough to hinder or completely undermine the new strategy before it even gets started.

It is important to keep in mind that most strategic expansions do not fail because of external factors such as market demand. They fail primarily for two reasons. First is hiring the wrong leader, but close behind is a failure of change management. Competitive practices play an important role in reinforcing behavior changes that are needed for the new strategy to be adopted throughout the organization. Regardless of how compatible the strategies are to one another, never assume adoption of new practices will be easy, and be prepared to focus time and energy into making collaboration a reality.

Wrapping Up

The right competitive practices are crucial to scaling execution of the competitive strategy and must be developed so they align with the disciplines. The Owner/Operator Dependent phase is often where the chief executive defines what they want those practices to be, while the Independent Operation formalizes those competitive practices through consistent policies, well-constructed processes, and tools that help both to enable the practices and to enforce them. The right policies, processes, and tools provide the necessary structure while, at the same time, providing a level of flexibility for innovation required in the fluid marketplace of staffing.

The right balance between structure and innovation varies between companies and is something that requires significant trial and error. As a company approaches Organic Scale, understanding the right balance is critical to maximize the potential of remote managers.

Achieving Strategic Expansion revolves around leveraging competitive practices where they are compatible while, at the same time, minimizing disruption to the legacy business. Even highly compatible strategies require extensive investment in time and money that should not be underestimated. Also, the less compatibility between strategies the more the success hinges on the abilities of the leader of the new strategy to create new competitive strategies while, at the same time, integrating both culturally and operationally into the legacy business. Competitive practices reveal much of the risk associated with Strategic Expansion by revealing the scope of the change management required. Without this understanding, it becomes much more likely for the leader of the new strategy to become isolated, increasing the chance of failure.

SUCCESS FACTORS FOR BREAKING THROUGH
THE DISCIPLINE OF EXECUTION

Figure 7.5

Transition	Execution
Building an Independent Operation	Implementation of sales and recruiting processes to define daily workflow and provide more structure to guide daily interaction.
	Review policies and limit exceptions to a minimum. Communicate and manage to the policies consistently.
	Implement tools to provide metrics that can be leading indicators of operational trends.
Achieving Organic Scale	Centralize training on competitive practices to ensure consistency.
	Encourage controlled experimentation at the branch level and discuss impact at monthly/ quarterly management meetings.
	Ensure corporate initiatives are relevant to the issues branches are facing. Make sure the branches have a voice before initiatives are rolled out.
Expanding Your Strategy	Identify what practices are truly relevant to the new strategy.
	Allow the new strategy time to develop and implement competitive practices that are relevant to their business.

BREAKING THROUGH

Chapter 8:
Are You Ready?

In the process of researching this book, we have had the opportunity to learn from extraordinary people who maintained a passionate commitment to growing their business through difficult times. We hope the perspectives shared in this book inspire you to pursue your vision for your company. This book is not just about top-line growth. It is about growing and building something exceptional. This means being able to walk into your business and see your vision realized by the company you have built and the employees you have developed over the years.

Breaking Through is just as much a personal journey as a professional one, and that journey begins and ends with the leadership team and, more specifically, the CEO.

This journey is largely defined by how the five leadership disciplines manifest themselves within your organization. To understand whether your organization is truly ready to break through, you need to honestly assess each of the disciplines. Below, you will find the definition of each leadership discipline along with questions you can ask yourself to evaluate the health of each one.

Leadership Disciplines

1. Commitment

The foundation of breaking through is built on leadership's commitment to build an exceptional company. Leaders who have the Discipline of Commitment are determined to grow and are willing to make the necessary personal and professional sacrifices that, while often painful in the short-term, are required for the business to achieve its long-term objectives. This commitment to growth is based on building an organization that is aligned with the personal values and priorities of the founder. For many founders of top-performing firms, growth is more than hitting a financial number; it is an integral part of their personal and professional legacy.

- Do you have a compelling reason why you started this business that others can relate to?
- Does that reason resonate with key leaders within your organization?
- Does your business purpose align with your personal values?
- Is there a company narrative that helps unite all your employees?
- Does that narrative provide compelling reasons why working for your company is a unique opportunity?
- Are you willing to make the necessary sacrifices to grow your business?

2. Direction

The Discipline of Direction is comprised of a clear company vision that is accompanied by a compelling strategy and supported by a well-aligned operation. As a company grows, the Discipline of Direction includes the ability to adapt the organization in an increasingly fluid and complex environment.

- Is your business driven by an intentional growth strategy, or is the growth primarily opportunistic?
- Can you name three to five characteristics that all your clients must share?
- Do you know what characteristics automatically disqualify a company as a potential client?
- Do you have a competitive differentiator that is embraced by your team and consistently executed? Can you articulate it in a sentence or two?
- Do you have the visibility to make educated management decisions?
- Do you have the resources (people, money, technology) to implement your strategy?

3. Culture

A focus on building a Performance-Driven Culture by design rather than by default was common across our top-performing staffing leaders. Most of the leaders we interviewed felt that their strong culture is a major competitive differentiator. Of course, culture has many facets and is difficult to define. At its core, we believe culture is a combination of a shared belief system and a common goal. Culture provides the unwritten rules of team behavior and plays a large role in defining how teams collaborate and focus on results.

- Does your culture drive behavior that is consistent with the needs of your strategy?
- Does your team have shared beliefs that reinforce the right behavior and help unite the team?
- Does your culture allow your team to have productive conflict focused on results?
- Can new employees be accepted readily into your culture?

4. Talent Development

The Discipline of Talent Development was a critical piece of the growth puzzle that we saw across the firms we studied. There was a significant focus on assessment, hiring, coaching, and promoting the internal talent needed to drive organizational growth. Many of the firms we spoke with have been members of both SIA's Fastest-Growing Staffing Firm list and SIA's ranking of the Best Staffing Firms to Work For. We find that the correlation between the two go hand in hand with the high-performance culture. The Discipline of Talent Development is especially critical in a service business like staffing, where growth is highly dependent on ensuring the right people are in the right roles and that those people are well coached on how to do their jobs.

- Do you have clear, measurable objectives for production and management roles?
- Do you have a proactive sourcing strategy to consistently identify new talent?
- Do you have an effective coaching program that both trains and motivates your team?

- Do you have clear criteria and processes for identifying and promoting future leaders?

5. Execution

Staffing firms that break through the barriers to growth do not accomplish it without relentlessly driving execution in their sales force and in their recruiting teams. The Discipline of Execution includes well-defined sales and recruiting practices supported by the right structure and strong leadership. Sales and recruiting are capabilities that require continuous focus and energy from leaders to ensure ongoing competitiveness.

- Do you have well-defined competitive practices for your sales and recruiting organizations?
- Are your competitive practices in line with your direction, culture, and talent development disciplines?
- Are those competitive practices effectively supported through the right policies, processes, and tools?
- Can local operations drive innovation and collaborate with other managers to replicate that innovation?

If you confidently answered yes to all those questions, then you are on your way to creating an organization that will break through. However, it is important to understand that the relative health of each one of these disciplines can become outdated or even deteriorate. Never assume that what you are doing today will allow you to compete tomorrow. You must have a healthy paranoia that your competition is improving every day, so you must improve as well.

This concept of continuous improvement or "kaizen" has been part of leadership theory for a long time and is one of the central drivers of innovation in manufacturing. While there are a lot of differences between manufacturing and staffing, they both live in a highly competitive world that demands incremental innovation driven by focused leadership.

Without a mentality of continuous improvement, an organization can fall further and further behind until incremental innovation will not be enough and more disruptive and riskier solutions will need to be considered.

Wrapping Up

Nearly all the executives we interviewed for this book found the journey to breakthrough growth to be among the most difficult of their lives. They also found it among the most rewarding. They were proud of the organizations and the teams that they had built. The rewards and satisfaction of that journey were more than worth the sacrifices.

We encourage those readers willing to take that difficult journey to dedicate themselves to their own improvement. Certainly, investing the time to read this book is one step. Next take the time to network with peers, establish an advisory board, and be open to outside perspectives to challenge your assumptions. The success of your company depends on the growth and development of you and your leaders. For your company to grow, your leaders must grow also.

While the journey is long and the challenges are many, we hope that we have shown what can be achieved by those willing to work at the necessary disciplines for breakthrough growth.

Good luck on the journey, and please reach out to us if we can be of any assistance.

Mike Cleland, *mcleland@chartedpath.com*
Barry Asin, *basin@staffingindustry.com*

Afterword:
Breaking Through in Action

As part of our research for this book, we interviewed more than a dozen leaders from high-performing staffing firms. These firms have been members of SIA's Fastest-Growing Staffing Firm list and have primarily grown from start-up to $50 or $100 million in annual revenue or more. This puts them in the top 2% of all staffing firms in the US. In the following pages, we allow the leaders of some of those firms to describe their journey in their own words as well as some of the major lessons they learned along the way.

Company Name:	Acro Service Corporation
Leader:	Ron Shahani
Year Founded:	1982
2016 Revenue:	$332 million
Company Focus:	Acro was launched to provide engineering staffing to the automotive industry and has grown into an international workforce solutions company, providing MSP; VMS; RPO; staffing across all categories; employer-of-record; and, other advanced services. Acro is also proud to be one of the nation's largest diversity-owned workforce solutions providers.

Breaking Through the Barriers to Growth: Nurturing the Team

Once we were in the $5 to $10 million in revenue range, I realized that if we were to continue to scale the business, we would need to nurture people more, encourage their ideas, become better listeners, and be more participative. That, along with a more team oriented decision making style, was the key to our growth.

You are only as strong as your weakest link, so you have to build up the capabilities of the whole organization.

Commitment: Move Forward or Fall Behind

I always wanted the company to grow. That's something I felt that if we don't keep growing, we'll fall behind. You've got to keep moving forward.

I also realized that in order to continue to grow, my success is directly proportional to the changes I make in myself and my ability to grow as a leader.

Direction: Strategic Breakthroughs via Hard Work and Persistence

I've learned that strategy is all about creativity. I'm not talking about creativity like Michelangelo but the creativity that comes out of hard work and persistence. If you do your homework on your competition and on yourself to help you understand your strengths and weaknesses, and if you are in the market, learning by talking to people, and take the time to put it all together, then you'll be surprised at the strategies you can come up with that will differentiate your business and help overcome your challenges.

Culture: Learning from Doctor Deming

In the early 1990s, I took a quality seminar with Dr. W. Edwards Deming, the founder of the modern quality movement. He told me that the day you stop learning, you are old! That really resonated with me, and from that day onward, I've sent everybody in my top management to Deming's class, and we became a very different company, very highly team oriented, and our growth really started to take off after that.

Prior to that, most of my experience had been in organizations that were run like the Army—just 'follow orders' kind of thing. Deming's style was a revelation and completely different, very participatory, and really emphasized that you are only as strong as your weakest link, so you have to build up the capabilities of the whole organization.

To this day, I still constantly talk about Deming's three sources of power: one is knowledge; one is personality; and one is your formal authority that you have in your position. A good leader never uses the formal authority. You use knowledge and personality, requiring you to continue to improve as an individual,

Ron Shahani

because if you want to be more knowledgeable, you have to read, you have to visit places, you have to have a worldview. And with personality, you've got to do all of that; you need to learn how to win friends and influence people. After that, I started reading self-help books and changing myself, trying to continuously improve in those areas.

Talent Development: Helping People to Succeed

Cultural fit is very important for our hiring. We have team interviews where the candidate is provided a set of questions in advance and makes a presentation to the entire team. We also have one-on-one meetings to supplement.

I realized early on that to grow, I needed to hire a team of people and trust them and give them the opportunity to succeed and help them succeed. That needs to become my number one priority, how to help my people to succeed and build a culture and environment for scaling.

Execution: Continuous Improvement

As Acro enjoyed rapid growth, we found that some existing processes could not meet the demands of increased scale. 'More of the same' became increasingly inefficient, and new processes had to be developed. Nearly all of the various processes involved in our business have been improved, streamlined, and automated by continual advancements in information technologies and Acro's ongoing development of software solutions.

Company Name: Advanced Group
Leader: Leo Sheridan
Year Founded: 1988
2016 Revenue: $152 million
Company Focus: Advanced Group began as an office/clerical staffing firm and has grown over time to become a mid-market focused staffing firm with specialties in office, finance, and healthcare as well as clinical trials, an RPO business, and a creative/marketing business.

Breaking Through the Barriers to Growth: Invest, Adapt, and Be Resilient

For me, it was never about how much money I could make in any given year but about how much I could put back into the business. That's been our approach since the beginning.

As a leader, you have to have confidence and even optimism that you have the ability to do something as well as or better than anybody else out there. Business leaders find themselves with market changes and conditions they won't be expecting. That is why adaptability and resiliency are so important. In 1991, I had my biggest customers leave because of the introduction of vendor on premise. That was one of those moments where I asked myself, 'What do you enjoy about your business?' That really got me thinking, 'Is there some other way to make a living while still doing the things I love to do in the space?' And that's why we researched getting out of the clerical commodity space and moving into more of the higher-end, professional niche staffing verticals.

Leo Sheridan

Commitment: Risk Taking and Ownership

Take risks, but don't bet the farm. If you really, really want to grow, you've got to take risks. Just make sure they are responsible risks.

We've created a cadre of owners through a phantom stock plan. That has been critical for us and has really helped drive our growth.

Direction: High-Touch Middle Market

Our strategy goes back to the early days of the firm, which is that we're a mid-market, relationship based business or non-VMS. Everything we do is retail transactional, and that's something that we have stuck with for 20 years. We build our business around face-to-face meetings because, for me, it's about that relationship. I don't think you build consultative relationships over the phone.

In order to scale, we needed a business model we could replicate easily. We focus on what we call 80/20. Since we have several businesses supporting multiple niches we needed to standardize our operational practices across all our staffing while allowing each niche to go a mile deep into their specific industry. This allows us to train managers to one business model and train producers on one process, one compensation plan with similar roles and responsibilities, and consistent KPIs. Our technology platform is the same across all the practices. Now we have our model almost like a Starbucks, meaning we just plug into a market and allow managers to launch it.

Leo Sheridan

Culture: Respect, Excellence, Accountability, and Leadership

Our culture has always been the same, with a focus on respect, excellence, accountability, and leadership. As a start-up, the culture is a by-product of the leader. At first, I was the player coach on the field. I think good leaders who build businesses are great coaches. They have a vision, but at the same time, they can help their people become successful. A good culture is a culture of winning, of competition, of being a good teammate, and of having high respect for the players and the team itself. We were always aspiring to do great work and, at the same time, keeping each other accountable. At the end of the day, you've got to win, and if you don't have the right players on the field and they are constantly dropping the ball, then you've got to respectfully make some changes.

As we grew and started building businesses in different geographic markets, I needed to really get my brain around how to codify the culture so that we can make sure that we hire to it and that we can clearly articulate what the culture is and how it manifests itself in the behaviors that people demonstrate every single day.

It starts with making sure you're clear on the vision, the mission, and the values. Then values are just ways to make sure people can demonstrate in their behaviors that they believe in those values. You need to make sure that you articulate the values, describe behaviors that support those values, and then translate those into performance management systems. Leader/managers are where the rubber meets the road. If they can't carry that torch every single day, then this is when things start falling apart.

Leo Sheridan

Talent Development: Been There and Done That

It's amazing how quickly you outgrow talent when you experience rapid growth. You can hire somebody for today to solve a problem, and because you are evolving and growing so quickly, that person might not be capable of doing the job needed two years down the road. I call them growth walls. Suddenly, we realize that we don't have the right people or the right structure, and we've got to change. That happens constantly. The other thing I learned while building new markets is that I prefer hiring people who have 'been there and done that.' The idea being that if someone has already built what you're asking them to do for you it dramatically reduces the risk of that person failing. The probability that the person is going to be with you four or five years down the road is much higher.

When you are $150 million and you have 360 employees and want to grow to 500, it's time to find a person to lead your people strategies. With the acceleration of our hiring, we needed to build a world-class training program in order to develop producers to profitability as quickly as possible. We've developed classroom and e-learning training systems and processes that now give us a high probability that people will be producing successfully within six months. This is a tough decision to make because the investment is huge. Either stay the course and have your managers coach to success informally or put a structured program in place. The issue as you grow is that, one day, you wake up and realize that informal and ad hoc training on its own is not going to cut it.

Leo Sheridan

Execution: Track, Measure, and Hunt

Early on, we were always looking to outside expertise to help us figure all this out. We've done many sales and performance training classes through the years, and we've gleaned a number of insights and strategies from them. Today I think what we've got to do is be much more sophisticated around how we share business intelligence and be transparent with our producers so they know where or how they rank, how they are measuring up against their budget, their goals, and their KPIs. We have a BI tool that sits on the top of our databases, and with a click of the button, you can see anything you want in your business, including things like rankings of the top producers, the gross profit for each business unit, and the like. We now can say to our people that we are going to track and measure their performance so that we can anticipate what type of results we are going to see. And if we don't get the results desired in a certain timeframe, we need to impact performance with training, coaching, and mentoring.

We've always been a sales driven culture and have always been about growth. If you take a mid-market approach, one key data piece we look at is how many new customers we are billing and measure how many new customers come in each week. That is the number one measure for me. With our strategy as a mid-market transactional retail staffing business, it means our sales activity needs to be really, really high. We've got to have hunters, people who are not afraid to work the phones and get out in front of customers. It takes a lot of energy to get one new customer, and we are asking people to bring in a lot of them because we don't have large client concentration.

Company Name:	ALKU
Leader:	Mark Eldridge, CEO and Founder
Year Founded:	2008
2016 Revenue:	$117 million
Company Focus:	ALKU focused initially on IT staffing nationally for ERP professionals. They have since added quality/FDA compliance and government/security clearance staffing.

Breaking Through the Barriers to Growth: Replicate Thyself

The biggest factor for us in our ability to break through the barriers to growth has been an unswerving focus on internal personal development of our team and process. We've managed incredibly fast growth over the past six or seven years, and we've done that based on hiring primarily entry-level people almost exclusively and then promoting from within. The benefit I see is that as these entry-level people become more knowledgeable, more senior, and better at their jobs, we should be theoretically working with an exponential growth factor. Today we have entry-level people right out of college coming in and plugging into this formula that we know works, but we also have seasoned people who are now performing at a higher level. It all boils down to the simple concept of 'replicate thyself.' And it's one of those things that I love about this business; I know of no other business where that simple concept of 'replicate thyself' is so easily put into practice.

I saw my job change more from $75 to $100 million than from $0 to $75 million.

Commitment: When Is the Time to Hire? Always!

From the very beginning, when we wrote our first five year plan, we realized that the biggest obstacle to our growth would be the ability to find, hire, and retain bright, motivated people. In fact, we have a saying that goes something like, 'When is the right time to hire a salesperson or a recruiter? Whenever you have found the right person.' From the very beginning, we focused on hiring revenue generating people whenever and wherever we could find them. We wanted to hire people who wanted a career, and the only way to retain people who want a career is to continue to grow as a company so that you can give them more opportunity.

That was put to the test in 2013, when by mid-year, we were trending below where we'd entered the year at. We decided to spend our way out of it, and it was a defining moment. We had a whole bunch of people to hire, and we were down in revenue, and we thought for a moment about whether we should really make the hires. Ultimately, we decided, let's move forward, and let's not do it halfway. Let's hire all the people we've signed up, and let's find others and hope that these new people help us get a deeper penetration of the market. We had a fantastic Q3 and ended the year up over the prior year. That was a defining moment for us in our commitment to growing the business.

If we are continuing to grow, there are always going to be some things that I should be reaching for and others that I should be letting go of. Sometimes I have difficulty understanding which is which.

Mark Eldridge

Direction: The Power of NO

It was in 2009. I remember we'd done a really good job for a client down in Texas. The client said, 'You could fill PeopleSoft jobs faster than anybody I have ever worked with. Can you help me with these dot net positions?' We thought about it a minute and ultimately said, 'No, that is not what we do.' We hung up that phone, and the three of us looked at each other and were scared out of our minds. Did we just make a mistake? We left work that evening saying to each other, 'If we need to, we can call him back tomorrow and tell him we can help with those jobs after all. Let's just think about it tonight, and let's try to fill some more PeopleSoft jobs.' And then I don't know if it was fate, but we came into work in the morning and all these other things that we were working on, specifically in the world of ERP, started to take off. We were busy and not sitting around wondering what to do with our time. Ever since then, we've been focused on ERP and realized that NO was one of the most powerful lessons we could learn about strategy.

Culture: Have Fun Working Hard

'Have fun working hard' is our motto, and I really do think that if you go back to 2008 and 2009, we thought for sure we were signing up for sheer misery, drudgery, and pain. Although there was plenty of that, we also got some fun out of it. Then I was totally perplexed. Why is this fun? I think that the comradery of having people who were working as hard as I was willing to work (and I was working harder than I ever worked before) and the respect that came from that

Mark Eldridge

were key components. Then knowing that if there's anybody that I want to be stuck in a foxhole with, it's these people. To have that feeling, that's what made it fun. Once we had that kind of defining moment, we knew it became about finding other people who would be intrigued by that and a sort of 'us against the world' stance that really connects with the right person.

Talent Development: You Will Work Harder Than You Ever Have Before
We only recruit right out of college and believe that it is much easier to get people bought into our culture that way. They also don't have any bad habits. One thing we focus on is being very clear with candidates for internal hiring that working for ALKU is not for everyone. They will work harder than they have ever worked before, and most people don't want to work here. They will have to make 100 calls a day, and 90% of the people who interview with us don't end up getting a job with ALKU. It's our way of making sure we get people who aren't afraid of hard work and who want to work for us. We also tell them that we won't call them back after the interview. If they are still interested after the interview, then they should call us back. And we tell them, 'Don't worry, you can't call us too many times!' That alone weeds out about half the candidates.

We also are big believers in process. We tell our people that if they work very hard and follow our process, we can almost guarantee them success.

Every problem can be solved through more clearly defined ownership.

Mark Eldridge

Execution: 100 Dials a Day

We are very focused on performance standards. Recruiters have to make 100 dials a day, 9 submittals a week, and add 12 new candidates a week to our database. Salespeople must make 150 calls a week and add 6 new hiring managers to the database each week.

It is very much an eat what you kill environment for us. People work on the orders that they can fill, and it is a free-market environment in that regard. There is also no cap on compensation, with most sales or recruiters earning 70% of their comp in base in the early years and 30% of their comp in base after they've become experienced.

Company Name:	Professional Personnel Service, Inc. and related companies doing business as an AtWork Personnel Services franchise.
Leaders:	David Luttrell and Marty Luttrell
Year Founded:	1993
2016 Revenue:	$98 million
Company Focus:	AtWork provides industrial, warehouse, and office/clerical skills to clients across Tennessee, Virginia, and Georgia as well as several other states.

Breaking Through the Barriers to Growth: Beyond Micromanagement

As we grew, we did everything there was to do in the business. We filled every job order and interviewed every person who came in the door. I was really a micromanager during those early days. I managed everybody to the greatest degree and realized that was not going to work and it was going to personally drive me crazy. So I had to step back, and over time we have refined our processes to allow for growth.

Commitment: Hiring Right, Accountability, and Vision

Growing the company comes from hiring the right people, holding them accountable, and making sure they understand what is expected of them and have a clear vision of the future.

If you want to continue to have a growth strategy, there is more security in it than assuming you will stay with a small operation. You can develop economies of scale when you have growth as opposed to a single-operation office. We also have something of more value that we can leave to our children.

David Luttrell and Marty Luttrell

Culture: Develop Your Internal Talent

As we became more and more stretched, we both realized that we needed another set of eyes on the day-to-day business. We hired senior management from outside the company. We hired people with the background to be successful, but we just didn't see the impact we needed from the role. We then set our sights on internal talent, and it became clear that internal promotion was the way we needed to go. Internal candidates understood our business, our priorities as owners, and they have strong relationships with the managers in the field. It has been one of the best decisions we made.

Talent Development: Inspect What You Expect

There have been two lessons learned. First is that micromanaging people does not work. You are not going to be able to keep your staff that way. Second is that holding people accountable is extremely important.

What you don't expect from people, you will not get. There aren't many people who work tremendously well without direction.

Execution: Driving Communication

To support our rapid growth, we knew our corporate resource team needed to provide greater support to the field. We decided to invest in HR, IT, and marketing. To maximize the return on each role, we have spent a lot of time and energy driving the communication between shared services and the field managers. We realize that it's great to have these resources, but the only way for them to maximize their impact is for them to understand the challenges of the field and work with those managers to build the right solutions.

Company Name: The Delta Companies
Leader: Jeff Bowling, Founder
Year Founded: 1997
2016 Revenue: $118 million
Company Focus: Delta originally focused on delivering physician search and, more recently, Locum Tenens staffing as well as Allied Health positions from its one office in Dallas, Texas.

Breaking Through the Barriers to Growth: Growing to Lead Leaders

There are three skills that I had to learn over time as a CEO. In the beginning, I had to be a good salesperson. Then after a while, I had to be a good sales leader. Finally, as we grew, I had to be a good leader of leaders. These are three unique skill sets, and not everyone wants to or is able to make those leaps.

Of course getting the right people in the right seats and making the right people moves over the years has been critical. Because what you need from your people on day one is not what you need at $10 million, at $15 million, or at $100 million. One of the toughest things I ever had to do was let go of a close friend who was great in the early days of the company but just could not grow with our business. That is the key to success, having the right people at the right time in the right roles.

Commitment: Ability and Desire

We had been operating as a lifestyle business owned by someone else. When the opportunity came to buy the business outright from him, I brought the top 10 people in our organization together and told them what the deal was—

Jeff Bowling

that we had to give away all our receivables and that I could not pay them right now. I did talk to the landlord, and I thought I could get 60 days from him. But anything we bill tomorrow, I can pay on. We had this tear-jerk, gut-check of a meeting, and by the end of the meeting, people were putting their credit cards in the middle of the table and saying, 'Let's go for it.' I get emotional still talking about it, but right then in the nanosecond, you understand that not only do you have a great opportunity, but you also have a huge responsibility because these people have put their trust in you and they believe in you. What drove me over the years was to always remember that moment when people said, 'All right, let's go. We are behind you.' That was the turning point. From that moment on, everything at Delta was very strategic. Things were done on purpose, planned out and proactive.

Our goal was to see how fast we could grow. How fast can we reinvest every bit of cash and not go bankrupt? Let's push this thing to the limit because we have nothing to lose. How fast can we go and not run out of cash? That was the strategy, and we wanted to get to a critical mass. We never wanted to be small, never wanted to be.

Everyone wants to grow, but for the firms that break through, I think the leader has to have the ability to think long-term, to chunk it down in digestible pieces, and to put the right people on the right things, and then stay disciplined to that over a longer period of time. It is key to have a five year plan and be able to execute on that, month in and month out, over that longer period of time. I think it has to do with ability as much as it does with desire.

Afterword: Breaking Through in Action

Jeff Bowling

Direction: A Disciplined Strategy

We were fortunate to land in healthcare and then in Locum Tenens. But we are also very disciplined in who we sell to and who our customer base is. We don't do much in the way of VMS; we don't do MSP or government work. Just because you can do something doesn't mean you should. With what we have, we still have less than 2% market share, and I just feel like there is so much runway left before we really have to get into areas that we don't know much about.

Culture: From Trust to Competition

We have four pillars of leadership at Delta: trust, coaching, accountability, and emotional intelligence. First is trust. You can't do anything until you have established trust. The next are coaching and accountability. And the fourth pillar is emotional intelligence. If you can do these four things, you can lead here. Build trust, hold people accountable, coach them, and then have emotional intelligence. The accountability piece is key, and it's not for everybody. Accountability consists of setting very clear expectations, which is much more difficult than people think. Most of the time, leaders don't set clear expectations.

I got my metric driven transparent style of management from baseball. My coach, Greg Dennis, taught me to be clear about where people stand and what their stats are. We posted them in the locker room on the theory that if people can see where they are at, they can use it as a catalyst for improvement. We are competition junkies. We used to have a family picnic; it's now called the Olympics. It has an Olympic-style opening ceremony, and it's a full day out of the office, with jerseys and uniforms. It's crazy, you put a game out here in front of our people, and they will kill each other over it. Often, someone has to have

Jeff Bowling

surgery after the event. That spirit is born from the culture that I and the other leaders in the organization created. Performance management is something that we really do well here, and it is born out of my baseball background and a real desire to compete and win.

Talent Development: Training like You Mean It

I'm an avid learner. I love to read and to get better. I'm not going to outsmart a lot of people in the room, but I can out-prepare them. And that's been my personal strategy most of my life, just out-preparing other people. That's why I really believe in training. Last time I checked, we did three times the amount of training that an average company in our general inside sales staffing space would do. It's hard for me to believe, but not a lot of people really value training. For some, it's just a necessary evil or an interruption to their day, and it's not embedded into the organization. We provide centralized training on topics like salesmanship, industry knowledge, time management, writing emails, and other very practical things. We even do things like how to buy a house for first-time homebuyers and how to be a better parent, because it's just built into the culture. We have sales clinics every day. You may not have to go every day, depending on your level and your recent performance, but we have these sales clinics, and they are practical, real world ways to get better at your job.

In order to grow leaders, you've eventually got to be okay with things getting done differently than you personally would do them. The key is to have some boundaries and guardrails. You want folks to have freedom and be empowered within those guardrails, but you've got to decide where those guardrails are. It is hard for a type A personality like me—and I think for a lot of leaders—to not be involved in every deal, to not have every idea and every solution. But the problem is, you can't just scale that. That's why I always say something I read in the Harvard Business Review one time, 'Do you want to be rich, or do you want to be king?' If you want to be rich, you've got to let your people grow and not be ruled over by you as the leader and king.

The least profound cliché in our industry is that great salespeople don't always make great sales leaders. I think it's a bit more complex than that. You must know why people were successful in sales to know whether they can be a good leader or not. So one of the other things you have to learn is how to identify talent. You have to identify sales talent who will be able to make the transition to sales leadership. There is a difference between someone who was successful because they had a cushy account versus someone who really had to work at it. You can't scale good accounts, and you can't scale somebody who just has an innate ability to sell. They have to know why they were able to go produce gross margin. That you can scale.

Execution: The Lost Art of Salesmanship

One thing we do really well is that we are very good recruiters. I believe salesmanship is a lost art, and if you can really outsell and out-recruit your competition, it gives you a huge advantage. We have been relentless on training our team to be the best recruiters and best salespeople they can possibly be.

Company Name:	ettain group
Leader:	Jeff Harris
Year Founded:	1996
2016 Revenue:	$150 million
Company Focus:	Based in Charlotte, ettain group focuses on delivering IT, health IT, and digital creative staff, serving both mid-market and large national accounts, some with VMS and MSP programs.

Breaking Through the Barriers to Growth: CEO Transform Thyself

I remember being $3 million in revenue and wondering how we were going to get to $20 million. And the same thing happened when we were at $25 million trying to get to $50 million. And even as we were approaching $100 million, we started to see the steam coming out of the pipes and we knew that we had to do things differently. As a founder, you always have to be wondering whether you are the person to lead the organization to the next level. You cannot be the same CEO you always were. You have to transform yourself. I have the mentality that the people who got me here are not necessarily going to get me to the next level. That includes looking at myself. You have got to be willing to make those tough decisions, all the way down, even to the people who were there with you from day one.

From $100 million to $150 million, we realized that in order to start planning and scale for the future, we had to have a recruiting methodology, career planning, HR, playbooks, and other things that the branches need to be successful.

Commitment: Work Ethic and Urgency

I worked for a large IT Staffing firm for a few years right out of school. One thing I took away from that experience was the kind of work ethic it really takes to compete in this industry and what I was up against to be successful. Without that experience, I don't know that I would have had the sense of urgency and activity expectations needed in order to be successful.

At some point, I consciously made the decision that I am going to become a great CEO of a bigger organization and that I'm going to go surround myself with external mentors who have done that. That was when I went out and built an advisory board. I asked them to shoot holes in my plan and challenge me to become a better leader. I also invested in some executive coaching to really do some very in-depth and very difficult 360 feedback on myself. And I also co-founded two industry peer groups to help each other grow and compete against the big boys. That really helped me validate and gain confidence in the things that we were doing.

Direction: Dominating Your Own Backyard

You have to make that decision. Are we going to try to go deeper into our existing markets and start taking on the MSP and the big enterprise, high volume, lower margin customers? Or are we going to stay with the mid-market strategy and continue to open up more branches? We went and embraced some of the big customers that we have. The biggest thing we did to be successful at that was to focus on being the best in our own backyard with the goal to get every major strategic customer that is a buyer in Charlotte. To make that work, we took some recruiters and put them on our large account team and created a delivery center and just started going after the VMS/MSP business. It took

Jeff Harris

a while to get that right, but we built a VMS delivery organization for those large customers and used that to go tell the story to everybody else, which led to winning some other really big customers

Culture: From Hustle to Values

In the early years, we had a culture of individuals who just hustled their tails off. The owners were right there with sleeves rolled up. People were having fun, and we just had this mentality that we were going to outwork the competition and do a very high-quality job. We also had a vision of creating opportunity for others, which is still our vision today. That was important to me, that we had this mentality and culture of self-sacrifice, where everybody helped each other and helped make somebody else successful. With a smaller, more controllable team, it was really out-hustling people that was making the difference in our success.

One of the biggest challenges as we grew, particularly as a founder and being so emotionally tied with what we are doing, was having to rely on my branch leaders to really be cultural ambassadors for us. Over the last few years, we had to really start implementing a strategy on leadership development for those frontline people to help them become really great CEOs of their markets.

Our culture of values are accountability, performance, attitude, respect, and teamwork.

Jeff Harris

Without a doubt, I would take every single person in our business—every single one of them—and start a whole different company by employing the vision and values that we have today. I think the culture is transferable, and it is the hardest thing to keep adopted as you get bigger.

Talent Development: What Got Us Here Won't Get Us There

The real fulfillment comes from seeing other people be a part of building something and seeing them promoted.

I think the most important and most difficult thing that helped us develop our talent was going to people who were leading our staff and telling them, 'I'm sorry, you are not the person to take us to the next level.' And we had to ask them to either leave or take less responsibility. We went out and hired some people who had industry experience. We've had to do that at every stage along our growth path. And each time, I had to have some difficult conversations with some great people. But what I've learned is that it always leads to an opportunity conversation for someone else.

Execution: Beyond the Wild, Wild West

As we grew, many of the sales processes were sort of the Wild West. The branches could do as they needed to get the job done. The biggest thing we controlled was the training. We had everybody to corporate, and we trained them on the same thing first, and then we sent them out to the branches.

Company Name:	Hire Dynamics
Leader:	Dan Campbell, Chairman and Founder
Year Founded:	2001
2016 Revenue:	$121 million
Company Focus:	Hire Dynamics focuses on commercial staffing in industrial, clerical, warehousing, and distribution skills primarily in the Metro Atlanta area and other cities within a six hour drive of Atlanta.

Commitment: Over-Hire and Find a Mentor

One thing I've learned along the way is that it is really important to over-hire for key positions. If you want to be a growth company, nothing can stunt your growth and your culture more than having key people unable to grow beyond their current level. I always try to hire two levels above what we currently need for key roles. There have been a number of times where people have outrun their capabilities as we grew and we had to let them go. That happened two or three times and really hurt our culture.

We had a board of advisors from day one and that has been a key contributor to our growth. Over time I began to lean more and more on peer groups like the independent staffing alliance, niche staffing alliance, and Visus that we joined. YPO (Young Presidents Organization) was invaluable and having mentors as well as getting involved in the industry by being on the board of the American Staffing Association (ASA) and attending SIA events. As you get bigger, the mistakes get more expensive so it's important to have advisors who will help you along the way. That discipline helped us to move quickly and to continue to grow.

After about $20 million, you start thinking about systems and processes. It is the same level as when you are closer to $100 million, but we had to have some level of consistency. You have to be clear on core values and reinforce. Simple is better and don't overcomplicate the business.

Direction: Find Your Tailwind and Focus

I remember, as we struggled to grow, talking with Guy Millner (the founder of Norrell). He said to me, 'Never underestimate the value of a good tailwind.' I took that to heart. It's very important to both pick the right strategy and execute well internally. You need to have both in order to have sustained growth.

We found ourselves at a point where I think one of our biggest mistakes was diverting from what we were really great at and not just sticking to our knitting in commercial staffing. We were at $40 million in revenue and woke up in 2007/2008 with four divisions doing everything from pharmacy staffing to finance and accounting to sales and executive search. That is where having an advisory board really counts, as they said to us, 'You are good, but if you are ever going to be great, you have got to focus.' And we did. While everyone else was going upstream, we went the other way and sold our pharmacy staffing. Even though we started in big four accounting firms, we had to admit that we were not good in finance and accounting. Once we focused, that was when our growth really took off.

I think it is impossible to over-communicate your vision or provide too much clarity of purpose.

Dan Campbell

Culture: Culture by Design

I remember seeing Fred Reichheld of Bain speak at SIA's Executive Forum. He was the creator of the Net Promoter Score. He said that particularly in service businesses like staffing, companies cannot sustain customer loyalty without first having employee loyalty. That really resonated for us as an organization—that we were going to put our internal employees first.

So much of culture is defined by who you hire, who you fire, and who you promote. If you don't have that part right, I don't care what your core values are; you won't have a great culture. Along that line, it was very beneficial to us in our early years when we got the whole senior team together in a room and said, 'We aren't leaving this room until we develop a list of the five non-negotiable qualities that we look for in everyone we hire.' We studied a lot of companies as we were trying to create our culture, and we modeled ours after Starbucks, Chick-fil-A, and Southwest Airlines, which were all very employee centric.

Talent Development: Best Resources Focused on Best People

We determined that if we are going to be an employee centric organization, then we've got to put our best resources toward getting good people and developing good people. That was difficult to do, but we took two of our top-producing people and put one in charge of all internal recruiting and the other in charge of training and development. That set us back financially about a year, but it's the best thing that we did.

Afterword: Breaking Through in Action

Dan Campbell

I think, early on, it's all about selling the vision to your people and recruits, because you really don't have anything other than a vision.

If you don't get the hiring right, nothing else matters. You can have the best core values, the best mission and vision statements, but if you aren't hiring to them, then you will never get any traction on developing the culture you want to achieve.

Company Name: LaSalle Network
Leader: Tom Gimbel
Year Founded: 1998
2016 Revenue: $56 million
Company Focus: With a focus in Chicago and San Francisco, LaSalle Network provides professional staffing and recruiting services with specialties in accounting and finance, technology, office services, call center, human resources, marketing, supply chain, healthcare revenue cycle, sales, and executive search.

Breaking Through the Barriers to Growth: No Sacred Cows

One of the biggest things I did that led to our rapid growth was firing that first seasoned recruiter who was my first hire when I started the company. After that moment, we really hit it big in terms of growth. That move led to a culture change. That sent a message that there were no sacred cows. You either produce and perform or are not going to be here. That was a big, big turning point for us.

We also used our move into new office space to make a statement. I had invested in the culture previously, but it's also about the physical space you are working in. The physical environment gets in touch with things that affect people's day-to-day emotions. In addition, once we implemented quarterly all-company meetings, it allowed people to feel a connection and helped fuel their commitment to grow the business.

If I had to change anything, it would be to have hired more people sooner. There are some big companies that will hire 10 people, knowing they are going to keep 5. I don't buy that. When I hire 10 people, I want to keep all 10. But it's key not to be afraid to fire somebody if they aren't making it. And in our business, if you hold people to metrics, the business will grow based on the growth in people.

Commitment: Lifestyle vs. Growth

The danger for CEOs is that they can often get caught up in having a lifestyle business versus really growing something.

Right after 9/11 was a key moment for us, where I grew as a leader and we grew as an organization. We had been planning to open a new office, but after the attacks, many people said it was too risky. I still remember that vividly, as I was only 29 years old. But I decided that if Chicago was a billion dollar market and it decreased by half, it would still be a $500 million market and I would still only be a $3 million company. I'd be silly not to do it. I am in the market share business. I am not a tech guy; I am a market share guy. So I said, I am going to do the second office. And I've had that office ever since. The people went out to run it and to grow it. The people I hired, many of them are still with me. It was the best decision, and it taught me that you don't want to be stupid, but you've got to have convictions. That move sent a message to the market, and then we really started to grow and continued our double-digit growth.

I gave a speech to our company, and I said, 'Listen, I have career motivations still. I am 44 and run what's viewed as one of the best companies in the industry, and I am not done. I have career aspirations. I want to grow. I want different challenges the same way you all do. And if I do that, then guess what. I've got to delegate some things to some other folks on my team even if some of those things may slip through the cracks.'

Tom Gimbel

Direction: The Value of PR

Our focus on branding and marketing always fit with our strategy of demonstrating our expertise as a professional services firm that happens to do staffing. Early on, I learned the value of PR. And ever since then, I've worked really hard to end up where we've gotten. Now we are on CNBC and Fox News, and in The Wall Street Journal, because we pushed the envelope with content that can be delivered and that validates us in the marketplace. A lot of businesses don't. In our business, it's a lot of penny wise, dollar foolish people. I believe that we are in this for the long-term, and we want to cultivate the soil and grow a lot of trees.

Culture: Upbeat, Electric, and Friends

When you walk into our office, you think that this place is electric. Our office has a really upbeat feel to it and is decorated like a dot com. We have bright colors; we have TVs on the walls and a wide-open lobby. Visually, you see bright lights and neon green. We also have a high interview volume with candidates walking around, so there is a buzz in the air. We really hire for culture.

It is not about hiring the right people; it is about firing the wrong people.

We have built our culture as a professional services firm that happens to be in the staffing and recruiting industry. When we go meet with the client, the last thing we talk about is what their openings are. The first thing we talk about is what their business is and what their challenges are.

Afterword: Breaking Through in Action

Tom Gimbel

One of the major misconceptions about business is that you shouldn't be friends with the people you work with. I don't believe that for a minute. I think you most definitely should be. Of course, there is still respect that goes to the person who is their boss. I've surrounded myself with people who can say anything to me when we are out for a few drinks, and then when we are talking about a business situation, if they can't convince me of their view, they follow my rule. And that's called business. I always say to my group that the good news is if you work at our company for a couple years, you can go get a job for more money at another place. No matter how much you make, someone will pay you more. The bad news is, you've actually got to go work there!

We celebrate the new hire date of every single employee and call it their 'rebirthday.' We have a party in the office with hundreds of balloons and the whole thing. Everybody gathers around and gives a standing ovation for the employee. It's taken on a life of its own. I give everybody a gift on their rebirthday, with the gift depending on how long they have been here. Now it's gotten to a point where my gift is not necessarily the best gift. Their teams have champagne or scarves for girls; men are getting ties or tickets to the Cubs game. One day— and I couldn't even tell you who started it, but I'm sure that it wasn't me—there were pictures taped all over the office of funny things that have happened to that person since they started working here. And, at least, the culture had surpassed what I as a founder could get it to be. And the people were responsible for it. To have a real birthday, you just have to wake up breathing. To have a rebirthday, you've actually had to contribute something to a team, and then you are appreciated.

Tom Gimbel

Talent Development: Training like You Mean It

We've been wrong and hired the wrong people. But one of the things I continually say is that it's not about hiring the right people; it's about firing the wrong people. We all make mistakes. You can't be a high-growth company and keep up with the growth and not make mistakes. The key is to admit them, fix it, and continue to grow.

We were named last year as one of the 125 best training organizations in the world. It's through a magazine called Training magazine, and it's Disney and General Motors and Dell and Starbucks and American Express and all that. I learned way back that if I can't hire people who already have the experience, and if I really want people to grow, I have got to train them. And we've got to really commit to it.

Execution: More Interviews Than Anyone Else

When we had a crisis early on, I started scheduling interviews at night and making sales calls during the day, and all of a sudden, our numbers grew. We had more candidates to work with. We were getting more motivated. And what we learned is that our big advantage is that we'll interview more people than anybody else does, all the time.

As an owner and CEO, never remove yourself too far from the sales process

Afterword: Breaking Through in Action

Tom Gimbel

Salespeople need to have two sets of clients. They need to cater to their internal recruiters, and they need to cater to their clients as well.

We focus on quality. I would rather commit to sending several candidates over in three or four days than four sendouts in 24 hours. The biggest complaint you get from clients is, 'People send me what I don't want.' We would rather wait a few days to find the right candidate.

Company Name:	Medix
Leader:	Andrew Limouris
Year Founded:	2001
2016 Revenue:	$170 million
Company Focus:	Medix focuses on providing specialized non-clinical staff in the healthcare space, with particular emphasis on healthcare, IT, and scientific positions across the US.

Breaking Through the Barriers to Growth: Transformation Over Time

We've gone from $0 in revenue, one office, and one person to 370 employees and $170 million in business in 14 years. The first five years were just 'stick your head into a phone and get in your car and run around visiting customers.' Back then it was 'the client comes first.' Everything the customer wanted, no matter what it was, you were there for them 24 by 7. I was the first one in the office and the last one to leave, because God forbid you leave the office and a client calls in when you are not there. After we hit the five year mark, every single year has been a massive change. Some of the people who got you to $10 million may not be the same people who will get you to $50 million.

Commitment: Failure Is Not an Option

When we founded Medix, we knew that failure was not an option. We didn't have a plan B. It was that kind of raw emotion that got us through our first years in business.

If you are going to scale your organization, it's kind of like an amazing football coach. If you are going to be the head football coach at the University of Alabama, then that's what you do. It is all-consuming. There are recruiting meetings all the time, and there are playbooks, and there's film. And everything you do is about the University of Alabama. Now, you love your family and your family absolutely comes first, but your family supports the University of Alabama; they are huge fans. I feel like that's one lesson because, at a couple points, I tried to separate family and work, and it doesn't work. You can't leave the business Friday at five o'clock and just go and then pick up the ball again on Monday. It's just not possible. I am not saying you can't have date nights and alone time, or not to shut off your phone and not get to sleep. You have to do all the healthy things to stay fit. But if you want to scale your business and build something that is amazing, it's got to be a top priority.

Direction: Get Focused!

I learned at one of the SIA events that I needed to get focused. Until December of 2008, we were all things healthcare. And then we shut down some of our businesses and put a plan together to say, who do we want to be? As a result, we got really niched. And we just took all those people doing other business and refocused them on areas where we thought we provided value. Now we have three lines of business: healthcare, scientific, and IT, all with a healthcare slant. Within those three lines of business, we have certain areas where we focus.

Culture: Medix Has Got Your Back

The things that we did for talent, the things that we did for our internal staff, and the things that we did for our clients were extraordinary. For example, a contractor would be driving to work and get a flat tire. It was natural for a couple of recruiters to go out to change the tire and buy the person a new tire. And that was in our DNA. During the early days in our company, my mom passed away. I went to the funeral in Greece. I got back, and I remember my team saying, 'Take

Andrew Limouris

all the time you need. We got your back.' Still today we have a saying here that at 'Medix, we got your back.' We talk about showing up for people in good times and in bad.

There is not one person in our company who does not know our core values. Our newest employee will tell you it is the desire to serve others; willingness to do what others won't; never, never give up; and locking arms to help each other achieve goals.

If you can clearly identify your core values and clearly identify your purpose and clearly identify your three to five year priorities and annual and quarterly priorities, then you know who fits your company, and you know who doesn't. Once you get to that point it's just, 'Let's go, let's run.'

Talent Development: Always Be Hiring

I started hiring people based on values. During interviews, I would turn over the resume and talk to them about everything but work. I would look for like-minded people I could work with 15 hours a day.

Never stop trying to find good talent. When you find someone, even if there is no opening in your company, hire the person.

To grow, you've got to hire people as good as or better than you and give them runway and collaborate with them. Don't be a genius with a thousand helpers.

Afterword: Breaking Through in Action

Andrew Limouris

Have an equity plan. Have something so that if the company grows, people benefit from the growth. It just makes it easier to have meetings and go through financials and do everything that you need to do as an owner of a business.

Everyone should have a coach or a mentor. I've had two during my time at Medix. We got a coach, and we started to follow their methodology. I think every team or any company should have a certain methodology in which they manage their business. One key to our success is that we never stop searching for that next coach or mentor. Once you stop learning, you stop innovating and you stop growing. You just kind of stop.

I try to read two books a quarter and find other ways to learn each quarter. It opens your eyes up to what's going on in the world. If you are not doing something every week to learn, you'll fail.

Company Name:	Signature Consultants
Leaders:	Jay Cohen and Mark Nussbaum
Year Founded:	1997
2016 Revenue:	$313 million
Company Focus:	Signature focuses on providing clients across the US with IT staff in a variety of skill areas.

Breaking Through the Barriers to Growth: Growth and Change

Your enterprise can't grow if your leaders won't grow.

You have to be able to stop and start all over again. There have been points at revenue of $50 million, again at $150 million, and now that we are over $300 million where we are just stopping and looking at everything. It has been key to our growth to have the willingness to start all over again if we are not getting where we want to go.

Commitment: Playing for the Long-Term

We were always driven by growth. Early on, and even today, we do not focus on short-term profits. We were aggressive about our growth because we wanted to invest in it. There is a mindset about wanting, thinking, and playing for the long-term, which leads to the willingness to invest versus making decisions designed for this week.

We have always been investing our profits into new markets—always. Our CFO came in two years ago and practically begged me to step on the brakes.

One of our things is to provide a place where people can join us and grow, not just professionally but personally. We put a big emphasis on personal growth. Two years from now, don't be the same person you came in as. Because if that is the case, then you've learned nothing. Even if you are better at sales, that's great, but how are you better as a person?

Culture

When we talk about culture, it's not about 'work hard, play hard,' as we believe that is just behavior. For us, culture is about our values and our stories that we tell to try to connect to our own history as well as our work ethic. All of that is what we are talking about when we talk about culture. It's also how we treat each other, the importance of being honest, and the importance of doing the right thing. Accountability is a very critical part of our culture. To us, it is doing what we need to do and, most importantly, doing what we agree that we should be doing. For our people, we all strive to do what we say we are going to do. Telling somebody we are going to do something and not doing it is lying, plain and simple. I think that's where accountability is. It's accountability for yourself and accountability for your partners that we all do what we say we are going to do.

Talent Development: Training Key to Growth

We never, ever wanted to lose a good person. We always wanted to be the best place for a consultant to work and the best place for our internal people to work. We never wanted to lose a client because of an issue of trust.

We really changed the company in the last five years. Prior to that, our training consisted of sending an experienced delivery person to a new market and then hiring salespeople there in those markets. Over recent years, we have

Jay Cohen and Mark Nussbaum

built a series of connected training programs that develop recruiters and sales people, so that for our existing offices we can fuel our growth and as we establish new offices we can provide the people who share our values, our model, and our processes.

One of the things that drove our unquenchable thirst for data was our inability to really help people improve, because we didn't know what they were doing. We would ask our early guys, 'Why are you successful or not successful?' No one could tell us, because they didn't know what process they were supposed to be doing. That was when we started putting in more refined data collection, before we started to really refine our process, and it was as we saw the data that we began to really understand. In 2010, we took one of our first recruiters and started a business development program and a training program. I think that if we'd done that earlier, we probably would be a billion dollar company now and would have grown a lot faster. Now over the last five years, we've developed a very real training program from the day you come in through becoming an established salesperson and we are working to take the program to later stages of people's careers in the next year or so.

Execution

Our philosophy since the beginning was to be a low guaranteed base, high-reward company. Our basic commission package has never changed in 20 years, though the bonus goals did change based on what we needed at the time. As a scientist, I've been gathering data since the first day. We didn't know what to do with it for eight years, but eventually it led to what we call Signature math. The math shows how each individual person can control their income, what they would make based upon how many submittals or job orders they had, based upon the typical ratios of that activity to results.

It's important to remember that we are dealing with people. One thing that really improved our performance with our candidates was when we forced our young recruiters to talk to our consultants. That was the only thing we changed, and it immediately turned around our Glassdoor rating, which had been consistently going down. Once we started talking more consistently with our consultants, our ratings started to rise. It happened because I believe that dealing with people made it a much more satisfying job for everybody; they weren't just placing widgets.

Company Name:	Strategic Staffing Solutions
Leader:	Cindy Pasky
Year Founded:	1990
2016 Revenue:	$321 million in staffing revenue plus MSP and International
Company Focus:	S3 provides staff augmentation, direct hire recruiting, workforce programs, and outsourced solutions with global industry expertise in energy/utility, healthcare services, insurance, communications, and financial services. It has more than 3,600 direct consultants in 49 out of 50 states in the U.S. and 11 countries including Europe and the Americas.

Breaking Through the Barriers to Growth: Profits with Purpose

We wanted profitability with a purpose. Our belief has also been that if we run a really good, solid business and we make decisions for the right reasons, then we will always have the resources and the capacity that we need to make decisions for people as well.

Commitment: Punching Above Our Weight

The reason I started the company is the same vision that drives us every single day. We feel that there are many ways to make money in this business, but if done right, you can also make a difference—not just a difference for our customers but also for our community, particularly in Detroit—and you can have customer relationships that are wide and deep and last for years.

In the beginning, there were no goals. The only thing that we wanted to do was make sure that we grew—and that we would never miss a payroll, that we were profitable, and that we were well thought of, both for customers and consultants.

We always wanted to punch above our weight. We weren't the biggest company around, but we always acted as if we were a level above where we ranked.

Direction: Focus, Focus, Focus

Our assumption was that there is always a market and you have to define it; you cannot let it define you. We decided we were going to develop customer relationships within the finance industry as well as the healthcare, insurance, and energy industries as our starting core. That focus gives us the ability to have a recruiting team that actually really does know the industry. We also get more references when it's industry to industry, because they admire you for the way you are doing it. This strategy paid off in 2008, when the banking industry crashed. We grew that year, and we grew within all our finance customers. Every one of our competitors in all of those customers lost ground. But we were in so many areas that we were going to grow and be part of the solution.

Culture: A More Generous, Caring Approach to Talent

When I started S3, I wanted a more generous, caring approach to how we deal with talent, a more flexible, creative approach to how we service customers.

Cindy Pasky

Culture is the fiber that weaves itself through every element of what you do as a corporation. We put our customers, consultants, and community first. We recognize that we need to be respected before we are liked. We are honest; we are ethical; we are ourselves; and we are very down-to-earth.

I think that, for us, culture gives us a way to define someone who may want to join the team in addition to the job and the comp plan. Our culture tells you what it is to be here: here are our values; here are our beliefs; here is how we do it; here is how we practice it; and here is why we think it's important. It gives us an avenue to be very serious but also to have fun. And then with our customers, it gives us an avenue for the customers too. When someone walks into a customer's site, clients know they are with S3 by the way they conduct themselves and what they say. When people interview with us for a job, by the time they get to me, they often say, 'I have spoken to eight people, and everybody said it a little bit differently, but I completely understand how they feel about this company and how this company feels about the way they should conduct themselves and the manner in which they should do business.'

What we really look for are people who are going to value the opportunity to be a part of S3, who get S3, and who recognize that they need to learn, want to learn, and are good people. And almost everything else you can teach.

Talent Development: Hiring from the Inside

It's really hard for us to hire from within the industry. Our best profile typically comes from looking internally. Is there someone who has earned the opportunity to have a chance to do this? Our second view is, if we are going

Cindy Pasky

to go outside, can we hire someone and teach them how to be a rep versus hiring someone with experience? Our last option is always to see if we can find someone who is experienced. That is a difficult hire for us.

There is really no set track for advancement. People have to be comfortable with that. We always say, 'If you work hard, a growing company creates opportunity.' It's really about how well somebody does something, and when they are ready to try something else, what's available? We have some level of formal training. We are very focused when we hire our sourcers and our recruiters, and we go to the recruiters; we don't have them go somewhere. So they are there to work with them.

Acknowledgments

The authors wish to thank all the people who helped contribute to this book during the actual process of researching and writing it, and those who, over the years, helped educate us in what works and what doesn't in the staffing industry specifically as well as business in general.

The process of writing this book could not have happened without the support of Marilee Cleland, who contributed many ideas, ruthlessly edited it, chased the quotations, and coordinated and managed the development of the book.

The team at Staffing Industry Analysts (SIA) all provided help and encouragement in various ways throughout the development of the book. In particular, Ursula Williams and Adrianne Nelson gave their enthusiasm for the topic and their numerous practical insights into the challenges facing staffing firms seeking to grow. Lorna Marengo assisted in arranging and transcribing interviews as well as confirming quotations. Jon Osborne provided many useful edits. Tony Gregoire, Jennifer Arcuni, and the SIA Executive team—Bryan

Peña, John Nurthen, Subadhra Sriram, Diana Gabriel, and Ursula Williams—all assisted with their support of the project as well as their perspective.

We would also like to thank the executives that took the time to share their experiences with us: Jeff Bowling, Dan Campbell, Jay Cohen, Mark Eldridge, Rupert Fordham, Tom Gimbel, Jeff Harris, Andrew Limouris, David Luttrell, Marty Luttrell, Mark Nussbaum, Cindy Pasky, Ron Shahani, and Leo Sheridan. Without them the content and concepts would not have been nearly as rich or as grounded in reality. Their passion for the topic has been a source of inspiration to us both.

A special thank you to Bonnie Daneker for her literary guidance, Carrie Wallace Brown for her design expertise, and Rick Leeson for his insight on funding company growth. Also, to the staffing leaders that previewed the book and provided feedback.

Mike wants to thank the leaders at MDI Group for introducing him to the industry over 23 years ago and providing him crucial experience he still relies on today as a management consultant. In addition, he would like to recognize all his clients for the opportunity to serve them as well as providing insight that made much of this book possible.

Barry wishes to thank Amy Asin for her patient and thoughtful comments on the concepts that intruded on many family dinners. He also would like to thank the staffing executives who mentored him and guided his thinking through his career in the staffing industry as well as at SIA, including Walt Macauley (who hired him in his first job in the industry), Jon Rowberry, Jack Unroe, John Bowmer, and Debbie Pond-Heide, among many others at Adia and Adecco. At SIA, a special thank you to Peter Yessne and Ron Mester for bringing him into the SIA family. Thanks as well to Chris Crain, the Crain family, and the staff of Crain Communications Inc. for their enthusiastic support of SIA and our growth plans through the years.

About the Authors

MIKE CLELAND

With over 20 years of experience in the staffing industry, Mike Cleland helps executives achieve their growth goals through leadership development and organization design. As the founder of Charted Path, Mike has worked with owners and executives on optimizing organizational structure, company governance, business planning, sales strategy, process improvement, performance management, and compensation plan development. In addition, he assists owners and investors with vetting and assimilation of strategic acquisitions. Mike has worked with over 75 companies ranging from start-up to $600 million in every major staffing vertical.

As a former president of a $60 million IT staffing company, Mike understands the practical challenges of execution and helps clients develop focused and feasible solutions that management teams can implement. When not working with his clients, Mike shares his knowledge through various articles, speaking engagements, and his first book, *Behind the Wheel: Driving Excellence in Staffing Operations*. Mike was named to the Staffing Industry Analysts Top 100 in Staffing for 2017. He is also an Everything DiSC and a Five Behaviors of a Cohesive Team Partner as well as a Certified Contingent Workforce Professional through Staffing Industry Analysts.

BARRY ASIN

A leading authority on workforce solutions worldwide, Barry Asin is renowned for his expertise on staffing and contingent labor. President of Staffing Industry Analysts (SIA) since 2010, Asin holds overall responsibility for the company's strategy, operations, and growth on a global basis. He has been with the company since 2003, where he previously held the position of Chief Analyst, leading the team responsible for SIA's award-winning research and content. He is a frequent speaker at industry events and is quoted in major business and industry publications, including the New York Times, BusinessWeek, Inc. Magazine, The Atlantic, Bloomberg Business, CNBC, Marketplace, USA Today, and MarketWatch among others. Prior to joining SIA, Asin spent nearly 12 years as a senior executive at global staffing leader Adecco SA. Before Adecco, he held operations management positions with PepsiCo, and he began his professional career with Andersen Consulting, the predecessor of Accenture. He holds an M.B.A. from Harvard University and a B.S. in engineering from Princeton University.

Endnotes

[1] Staffing Industry Analysts, Staffing Industry Analysts 2016 Economic Census Update Tool, August 2016.

[2] Staffing Industry Analysts, 2016 List of Fastest-Growing Staffing Firms, August 2, 2016.

[3] Staffing Industry Analysts, US Staffing Industry Forecast, April 2017 Update.

[4] Collins, Jim, *Good to Great and the Social Sectors: Why Business Thinking Is Not the Answer*, HarperCollins, 2005, page 31.

[5] Staffing Industry Analysts, 2016 List of Fastest-Growing Staffing Firms, August 2, 2016.

[6] Staffing Industry Analysts, US Staffing Industry Forecast, April 2017 Update.

[7] Staffing Industry Analysts, Staffing Industry Analysts 2016 Economic Census Update Tool, August 2016.

[8] Staffing Industry Analysts, The Lexicon: The Global Language of the Workforce Solutions Ecosystem, August 2017.

[9] Staffing Industry Analysts, US Staffing Industry Forecast, April 2017 Update.

[10] Staffing Industry Analysts, US Staffing Industry Forecast, April 2017 Update.

[11] Staffing Industry Analysts, Measuring the Gig Economy: Inside the New Paradigm of Contingent Work, August 2016.

[12] Staffing Industry Analysts, Measuring the Gig Economy: Inside the New Paradigm of Contingent Work, August 2016.

[13] Staffing Industry Analysts, Workforce Solutions Ecosystem: 2017 Update, Defining the Staffing Industry and Other Workforce Solutions, September 2017.

[14] Peters, Tom, *Thriving on Chaos: Handbook for a Management Revolution*, Harper Perennial, 1988, page 4.

[15] Greiner, Larry E., "Evolution and Revolution as Organizations Grow," *Harvard Business Review*, May–June 1998 Issue. Revised from the *Harvard Business Review*, July–August 1972 Issue.

[16] Maxwell, John C., *Developing the Leaders Around You: How to Help Others Reach Their Full Potential*, Thomas Nelson, Inc., 1995, page 92.

[17] Bennis, Warren, *On Becoming a Leader*, Accessible Publishing Systems PTY, Ltd., 2008, page 248.

[18] Kennedy, John, Speech of Senator John F. Kennedy, Raleigh, NC, Coliseum, September 17, 1960, American Presidency Project, University of California, Santa Barbara, http://www.presidency.ucsb.edu/ws/?pid=74076, viewed 11/1/2017.

[19] Treacy, Michael, and Wiersema, Fred, *The Discipline of Market Leaders: Choose Your Customers, Narrow Your Focus, Dominate Your Market*, Basic

Books, 1997.

[20] Branson, Richard, "My top 10 quotes on change," Virgin website blog post, February 6, 2015, https://www.virgin.com/richard-branson/my-top-10-quotes-change, viewed 11/1/17.

[21] Zook, Chris and Allen, James, *Profit from the Core: A Return to Growth in Turbulent Times*, Harvard Business Press, 2010, Kindle Version, Chapter 5: Growing from the Core.

[22] Zook, Chris and Allen, James, *Profit from the Core: A Return to Growth in Turbulent Times*, Harvard Business Press, 2010, Kindle Version, Chapter 5: Growing from the Core.

[23] Often attributed to Peter Drucker, http://quoteinvestigator.com/2017/05/23/culture-eats/, viewed 11/1/2017.

[24] *Office Space*, written and directed by Mike Judge, 20th Century Fox, 1999.

[25] Lencioni, Patrick, *Five Dysfunctions of a Team: A Leadership Fable*, Jossey-Bass, April 2002, page 195.

[26] Lencioni, Patrick, *Five Dysfunctions of a Team: A Leadership Fable*, Jossey-Bass, April 2002.

[27] Lencioni, Patrick, *Five Dysfunctions of a Team: A Leadership Fable*, Jossey-Bass, April 2002, pages 195–220.

[28] Naas, Roberta, "Steve Wynn Talks Luxury Jewelry, Reveals Plans for Giant Lagoon and King Kong in Las Vegas," Forbes, June 22, 2016.

[29] Alderson, Barnard, *Andrew Carnegie: The Man and His Work*, Doubleday, Page & Company, 1902, page 57.

[30] Staffing Industry Analysts, Largest Global Staffing Firms, 2017.

[31] Collins, Jim, *Good to Great: Why Some Companies Make the Leap... and Others Don't*, Harper Business, 2001, page 54.

[32] Staffing Industry Analysts, Daily News, "On Assignment Buys Apex for 600 Million," March 21, 2012, http://www2.staffingindustry.com/eng/

Editorial/Daily-News/US-On-Assignment-Buys-Apex-for-600-Million, viewed 11/1/2017, and Bernhardt, Gordon J., "Win Sheridan: Beginning With the End in Mind," September 2011, http://bernhardtwealth.com/Profiles/SheridanWin.pdf, viewed 11/1/2017.

[33] Insight Global Website, https://www.insightglobal.net/company/historycore-principles/, viewed 11/1/2017.

[34] Collins, Jim, *Good to Great: Why Some Companies Make the Leap... and Others Don't*, Harper Business, 2001, page 13.

[35] 60 Minutes, CBS News, "Pete Carroll's Winning Coaching Style," Interview with Byron Pitts, Produced by Cathy Olian and Joyce Cordero, December 11, 2008.

[36] Bossidy, Larry, and Charan, Ram, *Execution: The Discipline of Getting Things Done*, Crown Publishing Group, 2009, page 20.

[37] Discussion of blue ocean strategy, https://www.blueoceanstrategy.com/what-is-blue-ocean-strategy/, viewed 11/1/2017.

[38] Staffing Industry Analyst, Workforce Solutions Buyers Survey: All 2016 Reports & Cumulative Appendix of 2009–2015 Reports, March 18, 2017, page 240.